Contemporary Issues in
Police Psychology

Also by Jack A. Digliani:

Reflections of a Police Psychologist (2nd edition)

Police and Sheriff Peer Support Team Manual

Law Enforcement Critical Incident Handbook

Law Enforcement Marriage and Relationship Guidebook

Firefighter Peer Support Team Manual

Contemporary Issues in Police Psychology

Police Peer Support Team Training and
the Make it Safe Police Officer Initiative

Jack A. Digliani, PhD, EdD

To order additional copies of this book, contact:
Xlibris
1-888-795-4274
www.Xlibris.com
Orders@Xlibris.com
717940

CONTENTS

Introduction ix

Chapter 1 Police Peer Support Teams 1

Chapter 2 Police Peer Support Team Training 14

Chapter 3 The Make it Safe Police Officer Initiative 123

Chapter 4 More Reflections of a Police Psychologist 147

Appendix A Peer Support Team Brochure 163

Appendix B Psychologist and Recruit/Training Officer
Liaison (PATROL) 166

Appendix C Model Peer Support Team
Operational Guidelines 170

Appendix D Foundation Building Blocks of Functional
Relationships 178

Appendix E Diagnostic Criteria for Posttraumatic
Stress Disorder 182

Appendix F Critical Incident Management and the
Trauma Intervention Program 186

Appendix G Suggestions for Supporting Officers Involved
in Shootings and Other Trauma 192

Appendix H 25 Suggestions and Considerations for
Officers Involved in a Critical Incident 198

Appendix I Peer Support Team Limits of Confidentiality
Pocket Card 204

Appendix J   12 Irrational Ideas of Rational-Emotive
             Behavior Therapy 206

Appendix K   Helping a Person that is Suicidal 209

Appendix L   Comprehensive Model for Police Advanced
             Strategic Support (COMPASS) 212

Appendix M   Peer Support Team Code of Ethical Conduct 216

Appendix N   Examples of Police Peer Support Team
             Training Powerpoint Presentation 218

About the Author 227

References 229

Index 233

To my wife Lorie,
who fills my life with love and
makes all things possible.

INTRODUCTION

*C*ontemporary *Issues in Police Psychology* is comprised of selected material previously published in Reflections of a Police Psychologist and the Police and Sheriff Peer Support Team Manual. It also includes new and previously unpublished information. It is written for police officers and persons interested in policing. It is also designed to provide a single comprehensive reference and instructional resource for trainers of police peer support teams.

Contemporary Issues in Police Psychology is an independent, stand-alone document. Therefore, while familiarity with Reflections of a Police Psychologist and the Police and Sheriff Peer Support Team Manual is desirable, it is not necessary. Readers that wish a more comprehensive discussion of police psychological issues, police peer support teams, and the topics presented in Chapter 2, are encouraged to read Reflections of a Police Psychologist and the Police and Sheriff Peer Support Team Manual.

Information: Chapter 2

The *Police Peer Support Team Training* (PPSTT) program as presented in Chapter 2 had its beginning in 1986, the year in which the PPSTT was developed. The PPSTT program has been consistently evolving since then. The current PPSTT program consists of training in twenty-four core areas that are presented over four days. It has as its overall goal the development of basic skills in functional, lawful, ethical, and sustainable police peer support. Since its inception, hundreds of sworn and civilian members of law enforcement peer support teams have been trained through the PPSTT program.

The PPSTT program is considered one of several ways to train a police peer support team. It certainly is not the only way. It is however, a training program that has proven its value in many law enforcement agencies over many years.

Although it did not start out that way, the PPSTT is currently presented in primarily a powerpoint format. When this change was made many years ago, it helped to standardize the training provided to new members of law enforcement peer support teams. This assisted greatly in cases of area "mutual aid" where peer support team members of one agency were requested to augment peer support team members of another agency.

Standardization of basic police peer support team training is highly desirable. It not only provides similar baseline training for all members of police peer support teams, it also encourages a sought-after high-quality level of initial training. To this end, the International Association of Chiefs of Police Psychological Services Section (IACPPSS) developed and published police peer support guidelines. Within these guidelines, topics for "peer support persons" introductory and continuing training are specified. The recommended IACPPSS police peer support team training topics are: confidentiality, role conflict, limits and liability, ethical issues, communication facilitation and listening skills, nonverbal communication, problem assessment, problem-solving skills, cross-cultural issues, psychological diagnoses, medical conditions often confused with psychiatric disorders, stress management, burn-out, grief management, domestic violence, HIV and AIDS, suicide assessment, crisis management intervention, work-related critical incident stress management, alcohol and substance abuse, when to seek licensed mental health consultation and referral information, relationship issues and concerns, military support, and local resources (www.iacp.org). This represents a significant step forward in the effort to standardize police peer support team training. The PPSTT program as presented is, in part, an endeavor to further advance the standardization of police peer support team training. Although the PPSTT program preceded the IACPPSS training guidelines, there is a significant degree of topic overlap. This is because all police peer support team training must include essential support-oriented and field-appropriate subject matter.

The PPSTT selects from many possible training topics. The goal of the PPSTT is to provide new peer support team members with the fundamental knowledge and skills necessary to become a functional peer support team member. Other topic areas that are also important but not viewed as fundamental or are normally a component of basic police training are not included in the PPSTT. These topics are addressed or reviewed in ongoing and advanced peer support team training.

Much of the PPSTT program has application beyond that of police peer support team training. The core skills described in the PPSTT are as necessary for members of any peer support team as they are for members of police peer support teams. In fact, in February 2014, for the first time ever, a modified version of the PPSTT and the Police and Sheriff Peer Support Team Manual (resulting in the Firefighter Peer Support Team Training program and the Firefighter Peer Support Team Manual) were successfully utilized to train two newly developed firefighter peer support teams.

The Police and Sheriff Peer Support Team Manual and the Firefighter Peer Support Team Manual can be downloaded without cost from www.jackdigliani.com. It is recommended that the appropriate peer support team manual be used as a presentation and study guide in all initial police and firefighter peer support team training. After initial training, the manuals function as a review, reference, and resource document for police and fire peer support team members.

Also available without cost at www.jackdigliani.com are the Law Enforcement Critical Incident Handbook and the Law Enforcement Marriage and Relationship Guidebook. The Law Enforcement Critical Incident Handbook contains useful information for officers and spouses following an officer-involved critical incident. The Law Enforcement Marriage and Relationship Guidebook consists of helpful information regarding officer relationships. Both are useful in the ongoing training of peer support teams.

The use of the words *police* and *officer*, and use of the term *police officer* are intended to include civilian and sworn personnel of law enforcement agencies functioning at all levels of government. Also intended for inclusion are relevant military personnel and private sector employees of security and similar organizations. The use of the terms *police department* and *police agency* are intended to include all law enforcement and related organizations. The use of the word *spouse* is intended to include men and women in all relationships, married or unmarried.

For the most part, I have taken the liberty of using the masculine pronoun in sentences that require a pronoun. This permits the avoidance of the more descriptive yet more cumbersome phrases *he or she, himself or herself,* and so forth. I regret that the English language does not have a single pronoun that is inclusive of both genders. Rest assured that unless otherwise specified, the information applies equally well and is intended to include men and women. I hope that this style of writing, selected only for ease of reading, is viewed as nothing more than convention by female readers. Certainly, it is so intended.

Acknowledgements

Contemporary Issues in Police Psychology includes theory and practice information developed by many others. Their contributions form the foundation upon which much of the current work is constructed. In cases where the source of specific information is known, the source has been cited. The author acknowledges the contributions of sources and authors whose thoughts and ideas have been so thoroughly incorporated into general knowledge that they are no longer readily identified or cited.

Cover photo courtesy of Thomas Marchese,
www.ThomasMarchese.com

CHAPTER 1

Police Peer Support Teams

Many officers and police administrators have questions about police peer support teams. Some police administrators are unclear about the role of a peer support team, especially considering that most modern-day police jurisdictions provide counseling services through health insurance plans and Employee Assistance Programs (EAP). It is not surprising that some police administrators ask, "With employee insurance coverage and an EAP, why do we need a peer support team?" Good question. The answer is simple - peer support teams occupy a support niche that cannot be readily filled by either health plan counseling provisions or an EAP. This is because well-trained and highly functioning peer support teams provide support that is qualitatively different than that provided by health insurance therapists or EAP counselors. In fact, peer support teams provide support that is qualitatively different than the counseling of even the best police psychologists. The difference? The difference is the *power of the peer.* The power of the peer is the factor that is a constant in the support provided by peer support team members. It is the factor that is not, and cannot, be present in any other support modality. Therefore, if an agency wants to do the best it can to support its officers, a peer support team is necessary. Incidentally, a peer support team is one of the most valued resources for a police psychologist. Experienced police psychologists understand the power of the peer, which is the reason why many police psychologist counseling and proactive support programs are designed to incorporate the efficacy of peer support.

Some additional questions about peer support and peer support teams are presented and addressed below:

What is a police peer support team?

A police peer support team (PST) is a group of selected personnel (may include officers and civilians) (1) who are formally established and recognized as a peer support team in agency policy, (2) who have been specially trained in the principles of Level II peer support, (3) who function under agency approved operational guidelines, and (4) who provide peer support under the advisement or supervision of a licensed mental health professional.

What are the functions and goals of properly trained and clinically supervised police peer support teams?

Properly trained and clinically supervised peer support teams have two primary functions. They (1) provide peer support for officers confronting challenging stressors of everyday life and (2) serve as an essential component of the agency's response to officer-involved critical incidents. Members of high functioning peer support teams also assume a mental-wellness training role and participate in proactive mental-wellness programs.

The foremost goal of a peer support team is the enhancement of officer mental-wellness by engaging and applying the principles of Level II peer support.

How does a police agency start and select a peer support team?

There are several ways for an agency to initiate a peer support team. A full discussion of this issue is beyond the scope of this paragraph but suffice it to say that much depends upon the planned structure of the peer support team and the personnel rules of the agency. Many police departments seeking to initiate a peer support team start by identifying an interested officer and having the officer collect relevant information. Another way in which peer support teams are initiated is that an interested officer will approach agency administrators. The latter appears to be more common. (Most of the newly created police peer support teams seem to have been generated from the ground up, that is, they begin with an interested officer writing a proposal and submitting it to staff.) However, no matter how it begins, the interested officer is normally charged with the responsibility of gathering information about peer support teams and then presenting it to staff. The presentation normally includes information about the role of peer support, available peer support team structures, other-agency peer support team policy and operational guidelines, peer support team training, confidentiality and clinical supervision, anticipated short and long term costs, and peer support team state statute provisions (if applicable). From here, the department may decide to establish a steering committee (see International Association of Chiefs of Police Psychological Services Section Peer Support Guidelines at www.iacp.org) or move forward with a department-wide memo seeking those employees that have an interest in becoming part of a peer support team (During this time, work can begin on developing a peer support team policy and operational guidelines). Once those with interest are identified, a process to determine candidate aptitude, commitment, and credibility is developed. Many agencies require candidates (1) to be in good standing within the department (no discipline) for at least the past two years, (2) to submit a letter of recommendation from a current or past supervisor, (3) to submit a personal statement outlining the reasons the candidate wishes to become a member of the peer support team, how personal stressors are managed, and any previous training, education, and history that might be relevant, and (4) to complete a personal interview with a specially created interview board. (This process continues the assessment of interest - a candidate must be sufficiently interested to collect and complete the required documentation and participate in the interview). The department must decide who will comprise the board, but it is especially helpful to have experienced members of other-agency peer support teams included. A board of no less than three and no more than eight is recommended. Board members should be provided with any written material required of the candidates. Board members may also be provided with prepared questions to help standardize interview inquiries. These questions should be designed to assess aptitude, interest, commitment, and credibility. Allowing some time at the beginning of the interview for the candidates to tell the board about themselves has historically worked well. Peer support team interviews usually last for twenty to thirty minutes. Following the interview, candidates are rated by board members on a pre-designated scale. The scale can be something as simple as "no concerns - some concerns – major concerns." Board members then discuss their ratings and personal assessments of each candidate. Candidates are either selected for the team, placed on an eligibility list (if the number of qualified candidates exceeds the number of authorized peer support team members), or declined. Once peer support team members have been selected, a team coordinator is officially appointed. The team coordinator assumes administrative responsibility for team and becomes the contact person for all additional communication. After the peer support team policy and operational guidelines are in place, team members have been appropriately trained, and a clinical advisor or supervisor is on board, the peer support team can be launched.

How are police peer support teams launched?

Launching a peer support team is not difficult. For most agencies, the best way to start is with a memo issued by the chief or sheriff. The memo acts as a formal announcement that a department peer support team has been created and that peer support is now available. The memo should mention that team members have been specially trained and are clinically supervised. Most importantly, the memo should specify the confidentiality parameters of peer support team members and recipients of peer support. It is recommended that information about other available support services - like insurance counseling provisions, Chaplains, and EAP - also be included. This is because the memo should not only provide employees with information about the newly developed peer support team, but also offer a comprehensive review of all available support services.

In addition to the chief's memo, past successful peer support team launches have included a department-wide email message from the PST coordinator. Such a message further outlines the parameters of the peer support team and includes a "readiness to help" statement. Soon after the chief's message and the coordinator's message are distributed, selected PST members should visit all work groups and each shift briefing. During these visits, PST members present peer support team information, discuss PST confidentiality, distribute prepared peer support team brochures, and respond to any questions. The PST brochures normally include information pertaining to PST availability, PST contact numbers, a brief description of PST confidentiality, and some information about PST clinical supervision (see Appendix A). Peer support team posters including the names, contact numbers, and photographs of peer support team members can also be fashioned and posted throughout the department.

To keep department employees informed of peer support, many established peer support teams choose to publish and distribute a quarterly peer support team newsletter. A periodic newsletter is a great way to distribute relevant information and to remind employees of the availability of peer support (to view a peer support team newsletter visit www.jackdigliani.com).

Who should become a police peer support team member?

Police peer support team members may be sworn or civilian, employees or volunteers. As mentioned, peer support team members should possess an aptitude for supporting others and three primary characteristics: interest, commitment, and credibility. *Interest* - peer support team members must have an interest in helping others and an interest in the fundamental principles of peer support. Without interest, even the most skilled peer support team members eventually fail. Team members lacking interest are perceived by recipients of peer support as distant, inattentive, and uninvolved in the support process. Interest on the part of peer support team members is a vital component of functional peer support. *Commitment* - with interest, a peer support team member must have commitment: commitment to the ideals of peer support, commitment to the peer support team, and commitment to the recipients of peer support. This is expressed in the willingness to respond to requests for assistance at any hour and to function in compliance with peer support team policies and guidelines. *Credibility* - peer support team members must be credible. Credibility is established by ethical personal and professional behavior over time. The perception of credibility has a great deal to do with reputation. For example, it is not likely that an officer with a reputation for gossiping would also be seen as a person who can keep confidences. Therefore, officers with such a reputation lack the credibility necessary to become members of a peer support team. New employees should have at least two years of service before being considered for a peer support team. They will need at least this amount of time to become known in the department and to establish credibility.

Officers that function in an unofficial role of peer support (every department has persons like this - they are the credible people that others now go to for peer support) usually make good peer support team members following appropriate training...if they have interest and commitment.

What is Level II peer support? Is there Level I peer support?

Yes, there is Level I peer support. Level I peer support can be thought of as "traditional" peer support. This level of peer support is found in the everyday interactions of friends, co-workers, and others providing support to one another. Level I peer support is characterized by "friends talking" and sometimes "giving advice." It can consist of a one-time contact or ongoing interactions. For police officers, this level of peer support includes the *B and B* (booze and buddies) strategy for support and stress management. The B and B strategy for peer support has been around for awhile and is known to produce variable results. The outcomes of the B and B, like any Level I peer support, can range from effective to destructive.

Level II peer support has much in common with Level I, but there are some important differences: (1) Level II peer support is provided by members of an agency-recognized peer support team functioning within state statute and/or department policy and operational guidelines, (2) Level II peer support is provided by persons trained in peer support, (3) Level II peer support interactions are characterized by elements of functional relationships which encourage exploration, empowerment, and positive change, (4) Advice giving is avoided in Level II peer support - independent decision making is encouraged, (5) Level II peer support is guided by ethical and conceptual parameters – this makes it different than just "friends talking," (6) Level II peer support has positive outcomes as its goal – this is not always the case in Level I peer support interactions, (7) Peer support team members are clinically advised or supervised by a licensed mental health professional - this provides a "ladder of escalation" if consultation or referral is needed. A structured ladder of escalation is not available in Level I interactions, and (8) Level II peer support, while non-judgmental, includes a safety assessment – it has an evaluative component. If a peer support team member assesses that the recipient of peer support is dealing with an issue that exceeds the parameters of peer support or if it is assessed that the recipient is or may be overly stressed, depressed, or suicidal, the peer support team member is trained to act upon the assessment. This is accomplished by providing information about available resources, making appropriate referrals, moving up the ladder of escalation, or initiating emergency intervention.

Peer support team members capable of providing Level II peer support may continue to provide Level I peer support. Level I peer support occurs when peer support team members are not acting in their peer support team member role. However, when peer support team members are not acting in their peer support team role, the confidentiality privileges afforded to peer support team members during peer support interactions do not apply.

How are police peer support teams structured?

Peer support teams may be structured within a police agency in at least three ways: (1) coordinator model, (2) advisor model, and (3) supervisor model. The *Team Coordinator* (TC) model utilizes an appointed-officer peer support team coordinator. The team coordinator can assume any of the responsibilities specified within agency policy and the team's operational guidelines. The TC model is best applied in agencies where there is no or little funding. While not recommended, the team coordinator model is usually preferable to not having a peer support team. The most significant shortcoming of the TC model is that there is no program-endorsed licensed mental health professional providing clinical support for the members of the peer support team. Without such support, peer support team members are left to their own devices when providing peer support and are left to make decisions best made with professional consultation. The *Clinical Advisor* (CA) peer support team model utilizes a licensed mental health professional to advise peer support team members. The agency contracts with the clinical advisor to not only to provide consultation for peer support team members but also to meet monthly with the team to provide group supervision and ongoing training. The CA model includes the appointment of a team coordinator and can be established with modest agency funding. The preferred, albeit the most expensive peer support team structure is the *Clinical Supervisor* (CS) model. The clinical supervisor of the agency's peer support team is a licensed mental health professional who is either an employee of the agency or a contracted professional. The clinical supervisor assumes all of the responsibilities of a clinical advisor and additionally (1) accepts referrals from peer support team members and (2) provides direct counseling services to agency employees and their families without referral from the peer support team. The actual services provided by the clinical supervisor are determined by either a job description or elements of a contract. In fully developed CS models, the clinical supervisor assumes the de facto position of department psychologist (if licensed as a psychologist).

Why is clinical supervision of the peer support team necessary? It is not required by law.

Clinical supervision is intended to enhance the delivery of peer support services. It accomplishes this by providing for PST clinical oversight, supporting PST members, and functioning as a resource for PST consultation and referral. In Colorado, the statute that provides for PST member confidentiality, C.R.S. 13-90-107(m) does not require clinical supervision or a specific type of peer support team structure. However, to be protected under this statute peer support team members must be "functioning within the written peer support guidelines that are in effect" for their agency. Therefore, if an agency PST is not concerned about the protection provided by this statute, it would not need written guidelines. This is because *the statute does not require that peer support teams meet its standards*. The statute was intentionally written this way so that each agency peer support team interested in having the protections specified in C.R.S. 13-90-107(m) could develop written guidelines and comply with the additional elements of the statute in a way that best served their needs and available funding. Therefore, the statute serves the guidelines, not vice versa. When clinical supervision is required by the PST guidelines, it is because the agency has endorsed the values inherent in PST clinical supervision. This may not be the case in other states with PST confidentiality statutes. Peer support team trainers must be well versed in the PST statutory provisions (if any) for PST member confidentiality in the state within which PST training is conducted.

Are there different types of licensed mental health professionals?

Yes. In most states there are licensed social workers, licensed marriage and family therapists, licensed professional counselors, and licensed psychologists. Each license requires specific training, examination, and experience. To be licensed as a psychologist, most states require a doctoral degree. The other mental health licenses require a master degree.

Most states do not require a specific university degree or license to practice counseling. Unlicensed persons that practice counseling often refer to themselves as "therapists", "counselors" or "psychotherapists." There are no or few requirements to practice counseling as an unlicensed therapist, although some states now require that unlicensed therapists register in a statewide data base. The use of unlicensed therapists to clinically supervise police peer support teams is not recommended.

Psychiatrists are also mental health professionals. Psychiatrists differ from psychologists in that psychiatrists are medical doctors with specialized training in the treatment of mental disorders. Some psychiatrists practice counseling psychotherapy. Others specialize in biological psychiatry, the treatment of mental disorders with medication. These psychiatrists provide little, if any, counseling psychotherapy. Many psychiatrists practice counseling psychotherapy and will prescribe medication as needed. Psychiatrists and psychologists often work together. In such cases, the psychiatrist is primarily responsible for evaluating and monitoring any prescribed medication, while the psychologist provides counseling psychotherapy. Psychiatrists also work with licensed clinicians that are not psychologists. Psychiatrists will have an MD or DO degree. Psychologists will have a PhD, EdD, or PsyD degree. Currently, only a few states permit appropriately trained psychologists to prescribe medication for the treatment of mental disorders.

What are the "confidentiality of information" privileges of police peer support team members?

It depends upon the state and department policy. Several states have now enacted legislation that provides police and other peer support team members with defined confidentiality of information privileges. Some state statutes provide for peer support team confidentiality as "who may not testify without consent." This is the case in Colorado. This type of statute normally pertains only to testimony within the state court system. Therefore, in Colorado, peer support team interactions outside of the court system are not protected. To protect peer support team interactions outside of the court system, departmental peer support team policy must include a confidentiality statement.

Regardless of whether there exists a peer support team confidentiality statute, each police agency with a peer support team should include a peer support team confidentiality statement within its peer support team policy. Such a statement augments state statute (if applicable) and helps to clarify peer support team confidentiality within the agency. The statement can be as simple as, "Information

communicated in PST interactions is not subject to disclosure..."
"PST members are subject to all...disclosures mandated by law"
(excerpts from an actual Colorado law enforcement agency peer
support team policy). Together, these statements make it clear that
internal peer support team interactions are protected up to the limits
prescribed by law.

Peer support team policy confidentiality statements are
especially important in states that do not have a peer support
team confidentiality statute. In states that lack a peer support team
confidentiality statute, the only confidentiality protection available
for peer support teams is the policy statement. In these states,
the policy statement offers some peer support team confidentiality
protection within the agency, however it does not prevent the
disclosure of peer support information under subpoena or during
court proceedings. This fact must be made clear by peer support
team members in a disclosure statement. A disclosure statement
is comprised of information that specifies the limits of peer support
team member confidentiality - and should be utilized regardless of
whether there exists a peer support team confidentiality statute.
"Limits of confidentiality" information should be presented by peer
support team members to intended recipients of peer support *prior*
to engaging in peer support interactions. The intended recipient of
peer support then has the option to accept peer support under the
limits or to decline participation. In cases where peer support is
declined due to the limits of peer support confidentiality, the peer
support team member should provide referral to more confidential
support resources.

Police administrators should not be reluctant to include a peer
support team confidentiality statement in the peer support team
policy. The range of potential positive results produced by any peer
support team would be significantly narrowed without some degree
of peer support interaction confidentiality.

Whether or not there is a state statute specifying peer support
team confidentiality, there is currently no confidentiality of information
protections for peer support team members in the federal court
system. This is because the federal courts are not bound by state
statute. In a federal court proceeding, the information exchanged

in peer support interactions becomes subject to disclosure. This is important to remember because incidents involving municipal, county, or state officers move to the federal court system when there is an allegation of civil rights violations. In such actions, peer support team members can be compelled to testify. This is the reason that peer support team members should support officers involved in critical incidents, especially officer-involved shootings, *without discussing the incident.* While it is often helpful for involved officers to discuss their actions and experiences during and following a critical incident, such discussion is best left to state and federally protected confidential support persons such as spouses, attorneys, clergy, and licensed clinicians.

Who is qualified to train a police peer support team?

A licensed mental health professional with training and experience in individual and family counseling, peer support, critical and traumatic incidents, posttraumatic stress and posttraumatic stress disorder, substance use and addiction, depression and suicide, anxiety disorders, mental illness and diagnosis, grief and mourning, confidentiality, and Level I and Level II peer support is best qualified to train a police peer support team. Also, he or she should have at least some familiarity with the stressors of policing, an interest in police officers, and an aptitude for teaching. Qualified clinicians often team up with experienced officers and relevant others to present comprehensive peer support team training. Having experienced officers as part of an instructor team normally increases the effectiveness and perceived credibility of any police peer support team training program.

What does it cost to train and maintain a police peer support team?

The cost of training a peer support team depends upon the fee structure of the trainer(s) and the expenditure associated with possible employee overtime, travel expenses, classroom fees, and so forth. Instructional fees for qualified clinicians range from no cost (volunteer) to several thousand dollars. Many agencies have access to outside funding sources, thereby reducing or eliminating the initial agency training costs. However, for most modern law enforcement agencies, finding funding to train a peer support team is less challenging than finding well-qualified and experienced personnel to provide the training.

To maintain a peer support team in a manner recommended (CA or CS), the annual costs depend upon (1) which model is selected and the fees agreed upon by the department and the clinical advisor or supervisor and (2) department policy governing peer support interactions and overtime (for example, many agencies compensate PST members for attending scheduled meetings and training, and for providing peer support during off-duty hours). Individual agency peer support team training and maintenance costs may be mitigated by cooperating or combining with other agency peer support teams when appropriate.

CHAPTER 2

Police Peer Support Team Training

The *Police Peer Support Team Training* program is designed to train police personnel in the fundamentals of police peer support. Instruction beyond the PPSTT program is provided to peer support team members through ongoing monthly topic-specific training and annual advanced-program training. The monthly topic-specific training and the annual advanced-program training agenda is designed to enhance and extend the knowledge and skills of police peer support team members.

Monthly in-service training

Monthly peer support team training addresses two important aspects of in-service instruction: (1) periodic review of core topics, such as confidentiality and stage peer support, and (2) a discussion of new and timely topics. Periodic review of core topics is necessary because providing peer support is not the primary role of most peer support team members. Therefore, essential peer support knowledge and the appropriate engagement of peer support interventions naturally fade from memory. Review of core topics is designed to refresh memory and to cognitively reinforce the central principles of Level II peer support.

When not reviewing core topics, monthly training can focus on new and timely topics. These include topics selected by the clinical supervisor as well as those suggested by peer support team members.

One way to structure new-topic monthly training is to consider incorporating issues that have surfaced during group supervision. Another way is to address current circumstances within the department, other jurisdictions, and the world. Regardless of the topic or how it is generated, monthly training of new and timely topics should be presented and discussed in a manner relevant to peer support.

Although monthly training is the responsibility of the clinical supervisor, peer support team members may also assume a team training role. Team members that have special skills or that have recently attended specialized training can present instructional information within the monthly training schedule. Involving peer support team members as team trainers is an excellent idea. It engages members in team activities, helps them to solidify their knowledge, shares information with other team members, brings outside information to the team, and alters the less-than-desirable routine of consistently having the clinical supervisor as the training instructor. Monthly training is normally presented in a one to two hour block.

Annual advanced training

Annual advanced training is characteristically different than monthly training. It seeks to add to the knowledge and skill foundation of PST members in a significant way, and is the forum through which advanced peer support programs are presented. For example, one year the advanced peer support training topic was motivational interviewing; the year before that is was transactional analysis (TA). Transactional analysis training proved so successful that it was added to the core areas of the PPSTT. However, new PST trainers, if unfamiliar with TA, should consider excluding it from the PPSTT program. This is because the principles of TA, like those comprising all of the PPSTT core areas, must be made relevant to peer support. This is nearly impossible to accomplish for trainers that are not well-skilled in the theory and practice of TA. In any event, peer support team TA training should not advance beyond second-order analysis. Experience has shown that for peer support purposes, training beyond second-order analysis is unnecessary and tends to be confusing.

Advanced peer support team annual training is normally presented in a day-long, two 4-hour block (morning and afternoon) format and may include more than one topic presented by more than one trainer, Brief instructional programs provided by local experts, followed by a panel discussion of the presented material has been a successful classroom formula for PST annual advanced training.

Peer support team retreat

In addition to monthly and annual training, some peer support teams opt for an annual peer support team retreat. PST retreats bring peer support team members together in a relaxed and mutually supportive atmosphere. Retreats also allow team members that work various shifts to spend some time together. Although PST retreats provide an opportunity to discuss team administrative issues and often include a training component (usually provided by the PST clinical supervisor, a member of the peer support team, or guest presenter), the primary objectives of the retreat are stress decompression, team building, and just having some fun.

The Police Peer Support Team Training program

The PPSTT program is presented as an enhanced outline. It not only specifies PPSTT core topics, but also outlines what is presented *within* each topic. The PPSTT enhanced outline includes well-developed topic information that requires summary, as well as brief outline descriptors that require elaboration. Much of the information that requires summary is presented in the appendices. The use of appendices is necessary to avoid outline information saturation. Descriptors that are in need of elaboration rely upon the information included in other chapters and the appendices of this book, the Police and Sheriff Peer Support Team Manual, and the pre-existing knowledge of qualified police peer support team trainers.

While it is not possible to recreate a multi-day training program in writing, the enhanced outline will provide readers with an idea of the content of the PPSTT program. Hopefully, this will assist those that train or are preparing to train police (and other) peer support teams. However, as the normal flow of instructional information and trainer/ class interaction cannot be duplicated here, some readers may find the sequence of the outline or the transition from one topic to another lacking in continuity. This is unavoidable. It is the responsibility of trainers utilizing the outline to transform it into a fluid, interactive, and easily understood program. It is imperative that trainers remember that the enhanced outline is a condensed, abbreviated, and dormant representation of the PPSTT. Trainers must bring the PPSTT outline to life.

Information for peer support team trainers

Trainers should consider the PPSTT enhanced outline a descriptive guide. As a guide, it should be edited, altered, and adjusted as deemed appropriate. Similarly, qualified trainers should modify the PPSTT to fit their clinical orientation, professional experiences, teaching practices, and personal training style. The PPSTT works best when trainers add, delete, select from, and alter the presentation to best meet their training objectives.

Although the current PPSTT program utilizes powerpoint, it is not dependent upon any technological delivery system. However, if powerpoint or a similar technology is used in the presentation of the PPSTT, the trainer(s) assume the responsibility to engage class participants and make the presentation interesting. Experienced users of powerpoint know that simply reading from a series of text-only projected slides quickly disengages class participants. This is especially true for lengthy programs like the PPSTT. If powerpoint is used, the slides must be colorful, visually interesting, and topic-symbolic to achieve the best training result (Appendix N).

The acquisition of knowledge and the development of skills necessary to become an exemplary Level II peer support person are the specific training goals of the PPSTT. The acquisition of knowledge serves as the foundation from which skill-based behavior is generated. As class participants become more adept at peer support, they move beyond "good" or "satisfactory" to become exemplary. Exemplary does not mean perfect. It means being conscientious when engaged in peer support. This distinction should be presented and discussed during training.

Throughout the PPSTT there is an emphasis on learner self-enhancement. As class participants advance through the program, they are encouraged to implement program concepts that might improve their lives. In this way, they work toward self-enhancement, experience the benefit of positive re-conceptualization, prove to themselves that change is possible, experience the benefit of classroom peer support, and acquire the skills necessary to support others.

Trainers of the PPSTT must be prepared to go to where the class guides them, as long as class interests do not stray too far from the primary PPSTT program objective: prepare class participants to be exemplary peer support team members. Exploring class interests and incorporating them into the PPSTT program is a great way to present the PPSTT and to enhance the adult learning experience.

Philosophy, perspective, and experience

The PPSTT program, the police peer support team structure models presented in chapter 1, and the model peer support team operational guidelines (Appendix C) are representative of the author's philosophy, perspective, and experience. Other viable philosophies and perspectives are acknowledged.

Suggestions and comments

Suggestions and comments for trainers are presented in brackets { }.

The Police Peer Support Team Training program enhanced outline

The twenty-four core areas of the Police Peer Support Team Training program are:

1. Peer support
2. Peer support teams

3. Stressors and stress
4. Interpersonal communication
5. Conceptualization
6. Burnout and boreout
7. Family dynamics and issues
8. Mental health, mental disorders, diagnoses, and intellectual disability
9. Critical incidents, traumatic incidents, posttraumatic stress, and posttraumatic stress disorder
10. Concepts in critical incident exposure
11. Peer support team confidentiality
12. Confidentiality, clinical supervision and oversight
13. Foundations of peer support and intervention strategies
14. Model for peer support
15. Peer support tips
16. Alcohol, drugs, and addictions
17. Depression and suicide
18. Police officer suicide
19. Suicide by cop and officer witness to suicide
20. Police primary and secondary danger, the Make it Safe Police Officer Initiative, and police culture
21. Grief and mourning
22. Transactional analysis for peer support
23. Critical incident debriefing
24. Keeping yourself healthy

A pre-program Introduction and the material included within each of the core areas is described below. Trainers must assess and determine how much time to spend within each of the core areas. This is readily decided by considering several variables including (1) the topic, (2) the type of information presented, (3) a "reading" of class comprehension, (4) class interest and participation, and (5) the goals of topic presentation. Each core area must be made relevant to peer support.

Introduction

At the beginning of the PPSTT program appropriate introductions are completed, the Police and Sheriff Peer Support Team Manual is distributed, and the core training areas are identified. Following the Introduction, discussion begins with the core area of Peer Support and continues throughout the program until all core topics are presented.

1. Peer support

<u>Peer support, counseling, and psychotherapy</u>. Counseling - a professional relationship and activity in which a professional person endeavors to help another to understand and to resolve psychological and other life difficulties. Psychotherapy - psychotherapy is a form of counseling that is used as a treatment for mental disorders. It is the treatment of mental and emotional disorders through the use of psychological assessment, theory, strategy, and technique with the goal being relief of symptoms or personality alteration.

<u>What is peer support</u>? Peer support is a non-professional interpersonal interaction wherein a person attempts to assist another person with past or current psychological, emotional, or otherwise stressful circumstances and with whom they have some common background, experience, or history. These and other commonalities provide the "power of the peer" in peer support interactions. Positive peer support is best reflected in interactions wherein a peer has (1) successfully resolved similar issues or (2) is successfully managing similar issues.

<u>Brief history of peer support</u>. Organized peer support in America can be traced to the 19th century: Drunkard's Club 1870's, United Order of Ex-boozers 1914, and Alcoholics Anonymous 1935. Helper principle – the idea that one is helped by helping others.

<u>Level I and Level II peer support interactions</u>. Present and discuss Level I and Level II peer support.

Why peer support? Employee Assistance Programs and community mental health providers are significant resources but appear insufficient to provide the totality of support services which best serve those in law enforcement.

When peer support? Peer support is best initiated early in an officer's career. It begins in the Psychologist and Training/Recruit Officer Liaison (PATROL) program (Appendix B). {discuss PATROL and its "seeking assistance" stigma-reducing effect}

Peer support…listening, being available, being patient. Emphasis to class: "you already have the skills necessary to engage in positive peer support." {due to: aptitude, interest, commitment, credibility, and the support and communication skills you already possess}

Key points: definition of peer support, Level I and Level II peer support, PATROL, initiation of peer support, power of the peer, class participants already possess significant peer support skills.

Training objective: acquaint class participants with the concept of peer support.

2. Peer support teams

Peer support team structure and function. Peer support teams can be structured and designed to function in a multitude of ways. Most police peer support teams are trained to provide peer support (1) to personnel dealing with challenging stressors of everyday living and (2) immediately after identifiable high-intensity events (critical incidents). Critical incident intervention for PST members frequently involves on-scene support, continued peer support, and involvement in a follow-up debriefing process (if warranted). Peer support for the stressors of everyday living may involve PST members in a wide range of issues {trainer and class participants identify some possible issues}. The actual scope of support offered by any PST is determined by applicable statutes, department policy, and the department's PST operational guidelines.

Model for peer support teams: {discuss the following topics}

1. Team structure - coordinator, advisor, supervisor model
2. Agency PST policy and written operational guidelines
3. Criteria for selected peer support team members - aptitude, interest, commitment, and credibility
4. Specified confidentiality – statute, policy, operational guidelines
5. Clinical advisor or supervisor - support for the supporters
6. Monthly peer support topic training
7. Monthly group supervision – also as immediately needed
8. Consultation or availability of supervisor/advisor - 24/7
9. Peer support team as part of proactive support programs
10. Peer support team involved in police psychologist counseling program when appropriate
11. Peer support within specified team member policy boundaries {different from personal boundaries which are discussed later in the program}
12. PST member role in critical incident on-scene support, continued peer support, and debriefing (if any)

Good to know: (1) The efficacy of police peer support teams is in large part dependent upon the support of department administrators and supervisors. There is no "us vs. them" between department supervisors/administrators and the PST. We all have a job to do and a role to play. (2) Peer support team members are not union representatives. A clear boundary between the functions of PST members and union advocates must be maintained. (3) In order to remain in compliance with peer support statutes, department policy, and operational guidelines, PST members must know and periodically review these documents. PST members are held accountable by these documents.

Discussion of department PST policy, PST operational guidelines, and PST clinical supervision:

(1) Review of department PST and other relevant policy. If there are personnel in the class from multiple agencies, emphasis is placed

upon class participants knowing and understanding their agency policy.

(2) PST operational guidelines are discussed. Section titles of the Model Operational Guidelines are presented.

- Peer support parameters
- Clinical supervision
- Team coordinator
- Primary obligations (professional supervision, confidentiality, PST scheduled meetings)
- Duty to take action
- Clarification of role
- Availability and call out
- Compensation
- Debriefing
- Media
- Attorneys
- Outside agencies
- Team actions
- Referral
- Reach out
- Leave of absence
- Resignation from the team
- Removal from the team
- Compliance with guidelines

The rationale for the guidelines are discussed (rationale – to provide information about PST structure and function, to define expectations and responsibilities, to help PST members remain in compliance with statute and policy, to provide parameters for peer support, to assist PST members maintain a high quality of peer support, to outline confidentially and limitations, etc) (Model PST Operational Guidelines – Appendix C)

(3) PST clinical advisor or supervisor. Following a discussion of the actual PST model being utilized, trainers present information

pertaining to professional supervision and oversight, the ladder of escalation (ladder of escalation - the option of PST members to immediately contact their clinical advisor/supervisor with issues deemed critical and beyond peer support - the issue is moved up a "rung" in the support intervention ladder), and the availability of less-than-critical consultation (no need for immediate contact) when necessary. PST advisors/supervisors are also normally responsible for ongoing and advanced PST training, referral services, and providing support for PST members (supporting the supporters).

Officer-involved incident protocol: Presentation of relevant officer-involved incident protocols involving the peer support team (if applicable). Many jurisdictions have developed specific officer-involved incident protocols to be initiated under specified circumstances. These protocols frequently involve the agency peer support team. {if there is no established protocol, discuss how the department manages officer-involved critical incidents and role of peer support team}

Reach out: {discuss the following in a brief narrative} High-functioning peer support teams do not rely solely upon the initiative of others to engage members of the peer support team. History has demonstrated that many employees confronting known stressors are open to peer support but will not initiate a peer support contact. There are several reasons for this, ranging from lack of knowledge about the peer support team to an exaggerated sense of self-reliance. Recognizing this, peer support teams should include in their operational guidelines a reach-out provision. This feature permits peer support team members to take the initiative in cases where it is suspected that proactive peer support would be beneficial. *Reach-outs must not be intrusive, embarrassing, or be conducted in such a manner that they create or exacerbate a problem.*

Reach out and PST confidentiality - the act of reaching out is not confidential within the confines of the peer support team. A peer support team member can inform other PST members that he or she plans a reach out or has completed a reach out. This is necessary to prevent other PST members from unnecessarily contacting the same person. As one frustrated recipient of several well-intentioned PST reach outs exclaimed, "I have already been contacted by two other peer support people. I told them I'm ok. You guys should get your act together." However, if a person engages a PST member in a peer support interaction that was initiated through a reach out, that interaction and any following peer support interactions would fall under established PST confidentiality parameters.

Self-initiated Peer Support Activity (SPA) and Make a Contact Everyday (MACE): If PST members find themselves not being utilized or feel underutilized, self-initiated peer support activity (SPA) and make a contact everyday (MACE) should be considered. PST members can readily implement SPA or MACE without becoming a nuisance because most departments handle calls everyday which would warrant some form of PST contact. SPA and MACE contacts can be quite casual and must be non-intrusive. While SPA and MACE are types of reach out, they differ from a more formal reach out in that they may be engaged in the absence of a known or suspected stressor. When engaging SPA or MACE, keep it relaxed and informal, and don't overdo it!

Peer support team mission and responsibility: The peer support team functions as a support and debriefing resource for employees and their families. The peer support team provides support to personnel experiencing personal and work related stress. It also provides support during and following critical incidents resulting from performance of duty.

Peer Support Team Code of Ethical Conduct: Present and discuss the Peer Support Team Code of Ethical Conduct (Appendix M.) {emphasize item 6 of the Code - although it is not an ethical infringement per se to provide peer support to subordinates, PST members who are also supervisors must be vigilant to avoid role-conflict if and when they choose to peer support direct subordinates}

<u>Tools available for PST members</u>. There is an array of training, references, resources, and materials available to PST members.

- Basic PST training
- PST philosophy and mission
- Department policy
- PST Operational Guidelines
- Peer Support Team Manual
- Peer Support Team Code of Ethical Conduct
- LE Critical Incident Handbook
- LE Marriage and Relationship Guidebook
- State statute (where applicable)
- Monthly meetings and training
- Annual advanced training
- Clinical supervisor/advisor and clinical supervision
- Support from the PST coordinator
- Other PST members
- Support from family and others
- Officer-involved Incident Protocol (where applicable)
- Outside training, support, and information resources

<u>The future of police peer support teams</u>:

- Integrated into more police agencies
- Statutory confidentiality protections
- Standardized foundation training
- Standardized ethical parameters
- Clinical advisement or supervision
- Ladder of escalation
- Regularly scheduled team meetings
- Ongoing monthly training
- Advanced annual training
- Brochures, newsletters, posters, and retreats
- Shift briefing presentations

<u>Key points</u>. Structure and function of peer support teams, department policy, operational guidelines, clinical supervision, support for the

supporters, reach out, SPA, MACE, PST mission, Peer Support Team Code of Ethical Conduct, available PST tools, future of police peer support teams.

Training objective: provide PST information and outline PST member responsibilities.

3. Stressors and stress

The development of peer support skills begins with an understanding of stress. Stress is a multifaceted and complex phenomenon. It appears to be a factor for all living organisms. The concept of stress has its origin in ancient writings and has developed significantly over the past several decades. {discuss the following in brief narrative}

Stress: Hans Selye (1907-1982), an endocrinologist and researcher, defined stress as "the nonspecific response of the body to any demand, whether it is caused by, or results in, pleasant or unpleasant conditions." In this conception of stress, stress equals demand. A more contemporary and alternative view of stress maintains that the idea of stress "should be restricted to conditions where an environmental demand exceeds the natural regulatory capacity of an organism" (Koolhass, J., et al. 2011). Simply restated, in Selye's view the intensity of the stress response is positively correlated with the combined intensity of *all* current demands. Therefore, as the totality of demands increase, the magnitude of the stress response increases. In the latter view, stress is hypothesized to occur only when the demands exceed those of everyday living. Included in these demands are the biological processes necessary to sustain life.

The concept of stress differs from that of *stressor* and *challenge*. *Stressor* is the term used for the demands that cause stress. Therefore, stressors cause stress. *Challenges* are a particular type of stressor. Stressors that are perceived as challenges do not appear to produce the negative effects associated with stress. Instead, challenges are frequently experienced as re-energizing and motivating. Whether a stressor is perceived as a challenge or a problem is influenced by many factors. Among these are: type and intensity of the stressor, stressor appraisal, perceived capability to cope with the stressor, available support and resources, individual personality characteristics, and likely assessed outcomes. This is why a stressor that represents a challenge for one person may cause significant stress in another.

Stressor: a demand that initiates the stress response. Stressors can be thought of as psychological or physical, low to high intensity, short to long duration, vary in frequency, and originate in the environment or internally.

Fight or flight: a phrase coined by Walter B. Cannon (1871-1945) to emphasize the preparation-for-action and survival value of the physiological changes that occur upon being confronted with a stressor. The fight or flight response later became associated with the Alarm phase of the *General Adaptation Syndrome*.

General Adaptation Syndrome (GAS): (Selye, H.) the GAS is comprised of three stages: alarm, resistance, and exhaustion. *Alarm* is the body's initial response to a perceived threat and the first stage of general adaptation syndrome. During this stage, the body begins the production and release of several hormones that affect the functioning of the body and brain. During the *resistance* stage of GAS, the internal stress response continues but external symptoms of arousal may disappear as the individual attempts to cope with stressful conditions. In the final stage of the GAS, *exhaustion*, the prolonged activation of the stress response depletes the body's resources, resulting in permanent physical damage or death (http://www.ehow.com/facts_ 6118452_ general-adaptation-syndrome.html).

Homeostasis: "steady state" – an organism's coping efforts to maintain physiological, emotional, and psychological balance.

Overload stress: stress which is the result of a high intensity stressor, too many lesser intensity stressors, or a combination of both that exceeds normal coping abilities.

Deprivational stress: stress experienced due to lack of stimulation, activity, and/or interaction. An example of an environment likely to produce deprivational stress is solitary confinement. Deprivational stress is also the principle underlying the child discipline intervention know as *time out*.

The relationship between stress and performance. Stress increases performance up to a point. Once an optimal level of stress-for-performance is reached, any additional increases in stress will cause performance to degrade. Excessive amounts of stress will bring performance to a standstill.

The physiology of stress. The physiology of the stress response is characterized by increases in heart rate, blood pressure, respiration, blood sugar, and blood flow to the skeletal muscles. Additionally, pupils dilate, blood flow to extremities is decreased, and intestinal muscles relax. In general, the stress response "revs up" a person in preparation for action.

The person x event transactional relationship. The intensity of the stress response varies with the perceived intensity of the stressor; the perceived intensity of the stressor is influenced by one's perceived ability to cope with it. Therefore, persons can confront stressors that represent real dangers, such as a vicious dog, without any significant stress response if the dog is perceived to be friendly. Correspondingly, persons will experience a significant stress response to a dog they believe is vicious even though it is actually friendly. The intensity of the stress response in both of these "vicious dog" examples will vary with a person's perceived ability to deal with the dog. It is in this way that the stress response is said to be *transactional* (person X event).

The fact that we respond to our interpretations of our environment (internal and external) and our assessed ability to deal with particular stressors is a fundamental element of human experience. The best we can do is to perceive, interpret, assess, respond, and reassess. It is a fundamental limitation of what we can know and how we transact with the world.

Insights into the transactional nature of stress

Epictetus: (A.D. 55 –135) (1) "Men are disturbed not by things, but by the view which they take of them." (2) "It's not what happens to you, but how you react to it that matters." Epictetus was one of the first early writers to recognize the intimate and inextricable relationship that exists between persons and their environment.

Hans Selye: (1) "Man should not try to avoid stress any more than he would shun food, love or exercise" (2) "It's not stress that kills us, it is our reaction to it." (3) "Mental tensions, frustrations, insecurity, aimlessness are among the most damaging stressors, and psychosomatic studies have shown how often they cause migraine headache, peptic ulcers, heart attacks, hypertension, mental disease, suicide, or just hopeless unhappiness." (4) "Adopting the right attitude can convert a negative stress into a positive one." Selye is recognized by many researchers as the first person to specify the processes of biological stress. He is sometimes referred to as "father of stress research."

R.S. Lazarus (1922-2002) (1) "Stress is not a property of the person, or of the environment, but arises when there is conjunction between a particular kind of environment and a particular kind of person that leads to a threat appraisal." Lazarus maintained that the experience of stress has less to do with a person's actual situation than with how the person perceived the strength of his own resources: *the person's cognitive appraisal* and *personal assessment of coping abilities.*

Types of stressors. Stressors can be categorized in terms of intensity and duration. This simplified method of categorization can aid in the creation of appropriate stressor management strategies. Stressors can be thought of as:

- Low intensity – short duration (unwanted call from a phone solicitor)
- Low intensity – long duration (unfulfilling marriage or job)
- High intensity – short duration (most police shootings)

- High-intensity – long duration (prolonged torture or hostile captivity)

Frequency is also a variable for all stressors. Therefore stressors vary along the dimensions of intensity, duration, and frequency. Remember, stressors can be internal or external {present and discuss examples of the various types of stressors}

Occupational stress: stress caused by job demands. Each occupation is comprised of a cluster of *unavoidable* stressors. These are demands that are inherently part of the job. For police officers, interacting with non-cooperative persons is an unavoidable stressor. If not managed appropriately, occupational stressors can result in detrimental physical, emotional, and psychological responses. *Avoidable* occupational stressors may also become problematic when present in sufficient quantity and intensity. An example of an avoidable occupational stressor is a poorly designed department policy that fails to adequately address the issue for which it was written. A poorly written policy is an avoidable stressor because it could be re-written in a way that better addresses the reason for its existence.

Items for discussion. What are some of the unavoidable stressors of life? (examples – need for water, food, clothing, shelter) What are some of the unavoidable stressors of policing? (examples -confrontation, shift-work, working on holidays, coping with a chain of command, duty to protect others) What are some of the unavoidable stressors of your assignment? How do occupational and personal stressors transact? (for the most part they are cumulative – but work can also offer relief from home stressors and vice versa) Stressor management is really life management. Diet, exercise, and self-awareness are sometimes considered the big 3 of stress (life) management.

Two primary stress management strategies. (1) Change your environment (change for positive) and (2) change yourself (the way you think/feel about yourself, the way you think/feel about your environment, and the way you behave.) Changing yourself includes developing new skills to enhance your coping abilities. The first strategy acknowledges the ability to alter one's circumstances. The second strategy recognizes the internal and external transactional nature of human experience

Primary buffers against stress. Primary physical buffer against stress – exercise. Primary psychological buffer against occupational stress – the Occupational Imperative: *do not forget why you do what you do.*

Discussion. What coping skills are needed for police officers? *How to do the job.* Knowing how to do the job is necessary but insufficient for a healthy career. You must also know *how to keep yourself healthy* in your career and how to keep occupational stressors from negatively impacting your family.

Bio-psycho-social approach to peer support. Clinicians often think in terms of biological, psychological, and social issues when assessing and considering how to best assist a person. {identify and discuss some of the biological, psychological, and social aspects of life and lifestyle} How are these relevant to peer support? {solicit thoughts and experiences from class participants}.

Some things to remember: When confronting change and managing stress there are things that you can do that help – {those having special significance are in italics}

- *Watch how you talk to yourself* (relationship with self)
- Relaxation breathing-*breath through stress*-inhale nose/ exhale mouth
- Maintain a high level of self-care, make time for *you* {discuss the difference between self-care and being selfish}
- Keep yourself physically active, not too much too soon
- Utilize positive and appropriate coping statements
- *Anxiety: influence one part of your brain with another part of your brain* {by using self-talk and breathing exercises, reduce anxiety}

- Enhance your internal (self) awareness and external awareness
- Remember the limits of your personal boundary
- Practice stimulus control and response disruption
- Monitor deprivational stress and overload stress
- *Use "pocket responses" when needed/consider oblique follow-up* {a pocket response is a response that you keep in your mental pocket. They are useful when you're asked about something that you rather not talk about to the person asking. Simply use the pocket response instead of having to come up with an "on the spot" reply. Example: question -"What did you do out there?" Pocket response – "That was quite a call. I did my best. Thanks for asking. Sorry, got to run." "Got to run" is an oblique follow-up.}
- Apply thought stopping/blocking to negative thoughts
- Identify and confront internal and external "false messages"
- Confront negative thinking with positive counter-thoughts
- *Break stressors into manageable units; deal with one unit at a time*
- Relax, then engage in a graded confrontation of what you fear
- A managed experience will lessen the intensity of what you fear
- *Only experience changes experience, look for the positive*
- *Things do not have to be perfect to be ok*
- Stressor strategies: confrontation, withdrawal, compromise (combination)
- Remember: transactions and choice points = different outcomes
- Relationship imperative: *Make it safe!*
- *Work*: do not forget why you do what you do {occupational imperative}
- Utilize your physical and psychological buffers
- *Healing involves changes in stressor intensity, frequency, and duration*
- Use your psychological shield when appropriate
- Create positive micro-environments in stressful macro-environments

- *Think of strong emotion as an "ocean wave"- let it in, let it fade*
- *Trigger anxiety: "I know what this is; I know what to do about it"*
- *"Stronger and smarter"* (in combination with "Trigger anxiety" equals the "2 and 2")
- *Walk off and talk out your anxiety, fears, and problems* (walk and talk)
- *Being vulnerable does not equal being helpless*
- Develop and practice relapse prevention strategies
- Develop and utilize a sense of humor, learn how to smile
- *Things are never so bad that they can't get worse*
- *Do not forget that life often involves selecting from imperfect options*
- Time perspective: past, present, future (positive – negative) (Zimbardo, et al)
- Access your power: the power of confidence, coping, and management
- *Stay grounded in what you know to be true*
- Utilize the proactive annual check in and other proactive programs
- Keep things in perspective: keep little things little, manage the big things

Proactive Annual Check In (PAC) {proactive stress management}

1. Annual visit with the police psychologist, a member of the peer support team, or other support resource
2. Confidential meeting that does not initiate a record
3. No evaluation - It's a check- in, not a check-up
4. There does not need to be a problem
5. It's a discussion of what's happening in your life
6. Participation is voluntary and encouraged

Key points: stress and stressors, transactional nature of stress, life stress, occupational stress, unavoidable and avoidable stressors, occupational imperative, primary stress management strategies, primary buffers, and bio-psycho-social, some things to remember, proactive annual check in.

Training objective: provide an understanding of stressors, stress, and stress management; introduce proactive programs.

4. Interpersonal communication

Theories of interpersonal communication can be complex. A simple and useful way to think about verbal interpersonal communication is: Content, Message, and Delivery.

- Content: the words you choose in the attempt to send your message
- Message: the meaning of what you are trying to communicate
- Delivery: how you say what you are saying

Delivery can alter the message of the content. For example, how you say "have a nice day" might imply that you wish the person to have a nice day. However, if said sarcastically, it might mean the opposite. Many police officers have received citizen complaints wherein the person reported, "it's not what he said, it's how he said it." Nonverbal behavior including gestures and interpersonal distance (spacing proximics) can also alter the message of spoken content. {discuss significance of nonverbal communication}

All communication is relative to culture, era, and context. Cultural influences can define and/or alter the meaning of verbal and nonverbal communication. {discuss cultural differences in communication and introduce notion of cultural differences in general}

Communication Imperative - *a person will respond to the message received, not necessarily the message you intended to send.* {provide examples of how the same content can communicate different messages by altering the delivery, and how different content can send the same message}

Ten functional communication tips

1. Hearing is not listening. Be a good listener. This will help you to better understand others.
2. Remain relaxed. Pressured communication often results in misunderstanding.
3. Be mindful of content, message, and delivery. Use feedback loops when you're uncertain that your intended message was received and properly understood.
4. Remember that eye contact, facial expressions, and body posture communicate volumes. Issues: *validation* and *invalidation* of others.
5. Ask appropriate questions in an appropriate manner. This is a good way to show you are interested in the transaction. Avoid over-questioning and becoming intrusive - don't interrogate.
6. Try to understand other points of view. You do not need to change your beliefs or opinions in order to understand the views of others.
7. Avoid dominating or being a wallflower during the conversation. Seek a "participation exchange balance" in your interpersonal communication.
8. Don't immediately respond to something someone has just said by interrupting and then telling your story. For example, "We had a great vacation in Europe. We were able to see..." "Oh yeah. When I was in Europe it was great, I saw..."
9. Learn from your communication experiences. If a conversation didn't go well, change some things and try again.
10. Keep what works for you. Experiment with new strategies. Good communication is a skill to be learned.

Human complexity. Human beings are complex. Human beings are so psychologically complex that we have an ongoing relationship with ourselves (internal communication – self-talk). We also have a secret life. There are some things we know about ourselves that no one else knows. What concept do these factors involve? (self-concept) {discuss self-concept, internal communication, secret life, and "inner world"}

Key points: verbal and nonverbal communication, content-message-delivery, cultural influences on communication, validation-invalidation, Communication Imperative, communication tips, ongoing relationship with self.

Training objective: specify a working communication theory and improve understanding of interpersonal communication (later to be related to peer support).

5. Conceptualization

Importance of conceptualization. Conceptualizations are thoughts, beliefs, views, perspectives, etc. There are many ways to conceptualize. Most of our conceptualizations originate in childhood and come from significant childhood figures (this is why if you are religious, you are likely the same religion as your parents). Conceptualizations are important because they determine how we interpret "reality." This is the reason that a particularly colorful sunset is seen by some as nothing more than an atmospheric feature of an uncaring mechanical universe, while others view it as evidence of a beneficent Creator.

Some conceptualizations appear to be more functional than others. {discuss meaning of "functionality"}. There are also conceptualizations acquired in childhood that sometimes cause difficulties in adulthood. For example, being told by your parents that "you're stupid and you'll never amount to anything" can affect self-concept, self-image, and self-esteem in adulthood {provide additional examples}. The functionality of conceptualizations is measured against other conceptualizations (conceptualizations are relative). Conceptualizations represent the basic values of persons and what they believe to be true. Such conceptualizations are known as *core beliefs*. Core beliefs and other significant conceptualizations frequently drive behavior.

Sometimes we think about (conceptualize) difficulties in ways that create little opportunity for resolution. Example, "Life is bad...there is nothing I can do about it." Problematic issues must be conceptualized in a way that makes resolution or some improvement possible. ("Life is bad...I have to try something different or ask for help")

Cognitive psychology and self-concept. Self-talk, self-esteem, self-concept, values, irrational vs rational self-talk, thoughts and their effect on perception and behavior, core beliefs and their effect on perception and behavior. {discuss these concepts with class participants – solicit class opinions and comments}

Conceptualization and behavior. Model the behavior you wish from others. "You must be the change you wish to see in the world" (Mahatma Gandhi)

Attitude. What is attitude? (preconceived notions, perspective, personality traits, core beliefs, cognitive schema). How does attitude relate to conceptualization, life perspective, and behavior? {discuss}

Life perspective. A functional life perspective draws from the past (mindful of consequences and lessons learned) while maintaining a view of the future (potentialities and "eye on the prize").

Life management, life-by-design and life-by-default. Life management can be considered from one of two primary life perspectives: life-by-default and life-by-design. These perspectives are conceptual constructs and describe a theoretical continuum along which a person engages life. It is unlikely that anyone lives life totally by default or by design. Most people live sometimes or most times by default, and sometimes or most times by design. Life-by-default differs from life-by-design in that life-by-default is what you get if you do not practice life-by-design. Not much thought or effort goes into life-by-default. Persons who are oriented toward life-by-default often feel powerless. They subscribe to the *"This is my life. What can I do about it? It is what it is. What will be, will be"* life position. Life-by-default does not mean that life experiences are or will be undesirable. Quite the contrary, life experiences can default to very desirable circumstances. It is a matter of probability. The probability that life will default to something great and wonderful is less than the probability of desirable outcomes in life-by-design. The life-by-design philosophy is characterized by *"taking life by the horns."* Life-by-design does not mean that you will get everything you want. It means only that you feel you can effectively influence the direction of your life and that you are willing to act within your value system to bring about what is desired. Therefore, a person living life-by-design feels some ability (power) to make things different when desired. Remember, life-by-default is what you get if you do not practice life by design {it's worth repeating}.

Consequence and "prosequence". Consequences – results following behavior. Sometimes consequences of behavior are not well thought out..."why didn't I think before I did X." *Prosequence* – an idea in decision-making that encourages imagining that the likely consequence(s) of potential behavior have actually occurred and now must be confronted. *Prosequence* is thinking about what it would be like to have to deal with likely or eventual consequences of a decision. The idea of *prosequence* is useful in the effort to make decisions that result in more desirable outcomes. (example: imagining having to cope with the consequences of having an affair before you initiate one) {"prosequence" = coined word to help persons consider the likely or eventual consequences *before* they occur}

Key points: conceptualization, many ways to conceptualize, cognitive psychology, life perspective, life-by-design/life-by-default, consequence-prosequence.

Training objective: comprehension of the significance of conceptualization in human experience and personal perspective.

6. Burnout and boreout

Signs of police occupational burnout (many apply to burnout in all occupations and in all areas of life)

- A sense of dread, "nervous" stomach before shift
- Fatigue – feeling tired most of the time, no energy

- Easy to anger, irritability, lack of tolerance, lack of interest
- Low self-esteem, feelings of low mood/depression
- Negative outlook on life, life and/or job meaninglessness
- A sense of being trapped without options, "boxed in"
- Increased anxiety at work, in other environments
- Tension headaches, increased migraines, muscle aches
- Loss of appetite, stomach upset, eating disturbances
- Increased use of alcohol, nicotine, or other drugs
- Sleep disturbances, anxiety dreams/nightmares
- Sexual dysfunction: hyposexuality - hypersexuality
- Uncharacteristic behavior or "acting out"
- *Lack of concern for behavior consequences*
- Increased problems with coworkers/supervisors
- Increased family problems
- Increased citizen complaints

<u>Good to know</u>: for most of us, our job has components that are more desirable than others. Job burnout may result from too much focus on what you don't like, and not enough emphasis on what you do. The answer to job burnout is reclaiming your career. Consider what first attracted you to policing. Can you re-engage the thoughts and behaviors that were once rewarding? Find what you previously enjoyed about policing and re-engage those activities. Everyone needs to recharge their occupational batteries. Be creative to rediscover meaning in your work.

<u>Boreout</u>. Police officers, like those in other occupations, may also experience *boreout*. Boreout is a term first used by Swiss management consultants, Philippe Rothlin and Peter Werder (2008). They describe it as the opposite of burnout. Although deprivational stress is a part of boreout, being bored out encompasses more than just not having enough to do. It includes feeling underused and unchallenged.

Officers confronting boreout need to reevaluate their position, rewrite job descriptions, initiate new programs, develop new job functions, take on rewarding challenges, communicate with supervisors to address assignment parameters, expand job responsibilities, and similar to burnout - reclaim their careers. PST members must help others understand boreout. The answer to boreout (and burnout) is creativity.

The three-step answer to burnout and boreout:

- Reconceptualization - Cognitive alteration (occupational imperative)
- Creativity - Develop a plan or strategy (workable components)
- Reclamation - Behavior: engage plan (reassess and reengage as needed)

Key points: warning signs of burnout and boreout, getting back to basics, reclamation of career, use of creativity for improvement.

Training objective: relate the concepts of burnout and boreout to that of stressors and stress.

7. Family dynamics and issues

Marriage and relationships: two perspectives when approaching marriage. (1) There is nothing that we cannot work out, (2) if this doesn't work out, I can always get divorced. Which perspective is more predictive of marital success? {significance of conceptualization}

What are the stressors of policing that impact the family of police officers?

What can you do to help family members cope with the stressors of your job? (communication is important) {class input and discussion} (family issues often emerge in peer support interactions)

Functional Relationships. Foundation Building Blocks of Functional Relationships

1. Emotional connection
2. Trust
3. Honesty

4. Assumption of honesty
5. Respect
6. Tolerance
7. Responsiveness
8. Flexibility
9. Communication
10. Commitment

Spouses as "special status" persons (Appendix D) {present and discuss the Foundation Building Blocks of Functional Relationships and the idea of spouses as special status persons}

Intimacy, behavior, and sex. Intimacy is not sex – sex is not intimacy. Intimacy is an emotion and is characterized by a feeling of closeness and connectedness. Sex is a behavior. You can have either without the other. Fortunate people have sex with intimacy.

Behaviors within any relationship can enhance intimacy or create intimacy distance. Behaviors that enhance intimacy bring persons closer together emotionally. Intimacy distancing behaviors result in emotional drifting (loss of a feeling of connectedness) and disaffection. In highly functional relationships persons frequently engage intimacy enhancing behaviors (like writing love notes) and avoid intimacy distancing behaviors (like an extended silent treatment). {provide additional examples}

Intentional and unintentional harm. Some couples will intentionally harm one another. They do this psychologically, emotionally, and physically. One pattern of intentional harm involves playing the relationship *trump card*. The relationship trump card is played when a spouse implies or threatens to leave the relationship unless the other person does what is desired. This is different than being dissatisfied with the relationship and honestly discussing the possibility of separation. Playing the trump card is inherently manipulative and dysfunctional. It is intended to hurt, punish, dominate, and control. It is intimacy distancing and risks the relationship. It has several variations including, "If you don't do this, I'll leave" "If you don't like it, there's the door" "I'm not sure I'm coming home" and "Don't let the door hit you on the way out." The use of the relationship trump card is one level below the threatened use of violence, which is one level below actual violence, in the hierarchy of dysfunctional behaviors used to obtain what is desired in a relationship.

There are many relationship patterns and motivations capable of producing harm. Fortunately, most couples would not intentionally harm one another. Even if they become angry, frustrated, or disappointed with their spouses, most persons would not look to harm them in any real way. This is an important characteristic of most marriages. It has clinical significance for couples in counseling. If a couple would not intentionally harm one another, then it makes sense to think that any harm experienced must be unintentional. This realization can move a couple forward not only in professional counseling, but also in peer support and everyday life.

When considering unintentional harm, two points should always be kept in mind: (1) you do not have to intend harm to do harm (this is the very definition of unintentional harm), and (2) if you feel harmed, you should talk to your spouse about it. Do not let the feeling of being harmed, even unintentionally, build resentment or lead you to unfounded conclusions.

For the Foundation Building Blocks of Functional Relationships: two *foundation reinforcing rods*: (1) assume good faith in your spouse and (2) trust in the "lack of intentional harm."

Types of families. There are at least three types of families: family of origin (the family within which you grew up), immediate family (your family now, spouse and any children), and extended family (all family members including grandparents, aunts, uncles, cousins, etc). Concepts within family systems:

- Rules
- Myths
- Generational boundaries

- Alliances and coalitions
- Function vs dysfunction
- Homeostasis
- "Underflow" (the psychological undercurrents of the family system) {discuss and provide examples of these concepts}

Social interaction: Persons have differential desires (needs?) for various levels of social interaction: solo (alone time), couples (couple only), family (children, other relatives, etc), social/public (work, school, etc). Many persons do not get enough time within a particular level of social interaction. It can be challenging if one spouse is significantly different than the other (example, one person in the couple desires much solo time while the other desires a great deal of social/public interaction).

Relationship Imperative: make it safe. When it comes to positive social interaction in relationships, especially couples and family, remember the Relationship Imperative – make it safe. Spouses (and others) should feel safe to approach one another without undesirable consequences. (make it safe - cornerstone of the Make it Safe Police Officer Initiative)

Couples counseling. In couples counseling, it takes effort from both persons to obtain the most relationship improvement, but only one of the couple to put the relationship on a separation course.

Available for peer support team members to use and for referral - Marriage and Couples Exercise, included in chapter 4 and the Law Enforcement Marriage and Relationship Guidebook

Key points: Fundamental Building Blocks of Functional Relationships, intimacy enhancing-intimacy distancing, intentional-unintentional harm, reinforcing rods, types of families, family systems theory, levels of social interaction, Relationship Imperative, Marriage and Couples Exercise.

<u>Training objective</u>: familiarize class participants with relationship and family dynamics; introduce the idea of family systems; relate family dynamics and issues to peer support.

8. Mental health, mental disorders, diagnoses, and intellectual disability

To further understand stress and trauma - examine the concept of mental illness.

Concepts of mental illness, mental health, mental diagnosis, and mental disorder are presented and discussed. {the goal is to explain the current and historical conceptualizations of mental disorder. This is necessary for improved field assessments and a better understanding of the responses sometimes seen following critical incidents}

<u>Diagnostic and Statistical Manual of Mental Disorders</u> (DSM) (current edition: DSM-5)

- Briefly discuss the history of the DSM-5 (2013) (or contemporary DSM when DSM-5 is replaced) and diagnostic manuals (first DSM: 1952)
- The DSM is based on diagnostic criteria and not upon any theory or notion of cause
- Due to the complexity of the human organism and possible multiple disorders, proper diagnosis can be difficult
- Most mental illnesses are brain illnesses
- There are effective treatments for many of the major mental illnesses – but much work has yet to be done in the area of treatment
- Societal prejudice remains a significant problem for those persons experiencing mental illness
- The concept of insanity (not a clinical diagnosis - legal term pertaining to culpability)

Understanding mental illness. Provide a working definition of mental illness. Each state has a statutory definition of a person with mental illness {review state definition of mental illness}

What is a mental disorder diagnosis? Generally, a diagnosis represents a particular cluster of *signs* (observable behaviors) and *symptoms* (as reported by a person), often involves a "level of impairment" or distress, a period of duration and/or onset, and positive and/or negative symptoms. Brief review of the current major categories of mental disorders.

Some treatments for mental illness/disorders {review some historical treatments and control methods: chaining and confinement, spinning chair, ice baths, caging, strait jackets, pre-frontal lobotomy, etc}

Current treatments: Psychopharmacology   (medications), psychotherapy – many different orientations and strategies, electroconvulsive therapy and other electroceuticals (deep brain stimulation, transcranial direct current stimulation), psychosurgery, new age interventions, transcranial magnetic stimulation, others.

Understanding psychopharmacology. Many advancements have been made in the medications used to treat mental disorders (main effects). Medications have side effects – many undesirable. Some illnesses get much worse when the person stops medication. Knowing something about psychoactive medications can aid peer support interactions. Alcohol as a "medication" (complex diagnosis involving substance addiction and mental illness) {discuss main effects and side effects of medication – reasons for medication discontinuation}

Intellectual disability. The former diagnosis of "mental retardation" was replaced by "intellectual disability" (ID) also called "intellectual developmental disorder" in DSM-5. The essential feature of ID is significantly subaverage general intellectual functioning accompanied by significant limitations in several skill areas. *Degrees of severity*: mild, moderate, severe, profound. The degrees of severity are no longer based on IQ – now rated on adaptive functioning. It is possible for a person to be diagnosed with an intellectual disability and other mental disorders.

Key points: mental health, mental illness, DSM-5, diagnosis, insanity, treatments for mental disorders, psychopharmacology and effects, intellectual disability.

Training objective: comprehension of concepts associated with mental health, mental disorder, and treatment of mental disorder.

9. Critical incidents, traumatic incidents, posttraumatic stress, and posttraumatic stress disorder

Ever wonder why psychologists are so interested in your eating habits, how you sleep, and your sex life? (these are the systems most likely to be effected by stress and responses to critical incidents)

History of trauma conception. Traumatic reactions recorded since ancient times.

The influence of military psychology:

- American Civil War - irritable heart
- World War I - shell shock
- World War II - combat fatigue
- Korean War - zombie reaction
- Post-Vietnam War - posttraumatic stress disorder (PTSD) – Stressor(s) and symptoms meet specific criteria. PTSD is one of several stressor-related clinical disorders. {post-Vietnam because PTSD was not an official diagnosis until 1980}

Good to know: There are references to a condition that would currently be diagnosed as posttraumatic stress disorder included in the Iliad (Homer), believed to have been written around 800 BCE.

"...it is strange to think how to this very day I cannot sleep a night without great terrors of the fire; and this very night could not sleep to almost two in the morning through thoughts of the fire." Samuel Pepys (1633-1703) after the London fire of 1666.

Critical incidents: Critical incidents are characteristically different from the stressors of everyday life. While the circumstances of everyday life can be stressful, critical incidents are those that lie outside the norm of common experience. Critical incidents are often unexpected, high in intensity, and have the potential to overwhelm normal coping mechanisms. They often represent a threat to the safety and welfare of self or others. They may involve injury, death, or near death. The nature of a critical incident has the potential to traumatize those involved.

Summary of critical incident characteristics -

- Often sudden, unexpected, and high intensity
- Involves loss or threat of loss of life to self or others
- Disrupts core beliefs or the conception of "how the world works"
- Potentially overwhelming for normal ego defense mechanisms - can strip personal defense mechanisms
- Commonly involves *in-progress* altered perceptual phenomenon
- "One-shot" learning (classical conditioning associations that do not require repeated pairings – effect is due to the intensity of the stressor or event)
- Can cause lifetime physiological dysregulation
- Can turn the *person-in-the-world* upside down
- Can be comprised of repeated and cumulative exposures

Perceptual Distortions Reported Experienced During a Critical Incident.

1. Slow motion
2. Fast motion
3. Muted/diminished sounds
4. Amplified sounds

5. Slowing of time
6. Accelerated time
7. Dissociation
8. Tunnel vision
9. Heightened visual clarity
10. Vivid images
11. "Automatic pilot"
12. Memory loss for part of event
13. Memory loss for part of your actions
14. False memory
15. Temporary paralysis (Christensen & Artwohl, (1997) & Digliani, 2015)

Common Responses Following a Traumatic Incident

heightened sense of danger - fear and anxiety
splitting of environments (work/non-work)
anger, frustration, and blaming
super-conditioned learning (surface lesson/depth lesson)
isolation, withdrawal, and alienation
sleep difficulties - insomnia or hypersomnia, dreams and nightmares
intrusive thoughts - obsessive thinking, preoccupation with incident,
     endless video phenomenon
emotional numbing - avoidance/withdrawal
depression/guilt
desire difficulties - sexual, eating appetite
second guessing
interpersonal difficulties - family and friends, work and authority figures
alcohol and drug abuse - self-medication, prescription/street drugs
grief and mourning - complicated bereavement

Factors Affecting Magnitude of Response.

Person Variables

1. History
2. Personality

3. View of reality
4. Beliefs and aforethought
5. Assessment of threat
6. Assessment of performance
7. Assessment of options
8. Stress training and coping abilities

Incident Variables

1. Proximity
2. Sudden or planned
3. Blood and gore
4. Age of others
5. Personal history of suspect
6. Suspect or others behavior
7. Alone or with other officers
8. Circumstances of the event

Critical incident considerations: levels of decompensation

1. *possible*: no or very little reaction

2. *likely*: some degree of decompensation

3. *most decompensated*: psychotic reactions, severe posttraumatic stress disorder

Ultimate Survivor video: Case of Steve Chaney (Caliber Press) {presentation of officer-involved critical incident dated from the 1970s - remains timely and appropriate. May be presented elsewhere within this block at discretion of trainer}

Critical incidents and trauma. Involvement in a critical incident can cause varying degrees of psychological trauma. This is because the actual outcome for a person who has been involved in a critical event is determined by the complex transaction of event circumstances, personal characteristics, and the perceived elements of the incident.

Critical incidents and traumatic incidents. Some incidents that appear critical when viewed from the outside (like an officer involved injury or shooting) may cause no or little psychological trauma to those involved. Conversely, some incidents that appear non-critical may cause significant psychological trauma. Another way of thinking about this is that "critical" is a feature of the incident, while "trauma" is a concept associated with human (and other organism) experience. This is why two officers involved in the same critical incident in very similar ways can experience different degrees of individual trauma. Simply stated, any incident, whether or not it appears "critical" to an outside observer, may traumatize one or all of those involved. This is because the concept of "critical" is relative and dynamic.

The degree of traumatization following a critical incident can range from no or insignificant distress to a constellation of physiological, psychological, and sociological symptoms and impairment collectively diagnosed as posttraumatic stress disorder (PTSD) or other stressor-related disorder. This is the difference between critical incidents and traumatic incidents – the same critical incident may become a traumatic incident for some of those involved and not for others.

Posttraumatic stress and posttraumatic stress disorder. *Posttraumatic stress* (PTS) - expected and predictable responses to a critical incident. Normally resolves within a month through the person's resources and outside psychological support. In PTS, there is no clinically significant distress or impairment. *Posttraumatic stress disorder* - a constellation of clinical symptoms which meet specific criteria for the PTSD diagnosis, including clinically significant distress or impairment. PTSD is best addressed with professional treatment. The symptoms of PTSD may last months or years. Lifetime PTSD and other incident-initiated mental disorders, such as depression and anxiety disorders, are also possible.

PTS and PTSD may include atypical visual hallucinations. {not as uncommon as previously thought – such phenomena are subject to various interpretations by those that experience them – influence of personal conceptualizations and core beliefs}

Posttraumatic stress disorder (DSM-5). {PTSD diagnostic criteria is presented - Appendix E}

Summary of PTSD criteria:

- Exposure: stressor(s)
- Intrusion
- Avoidance
- Negative alterations in cognitions and mood
- Alterations in arousal and reactivity
- Duration: more than one month
- Distress or impairment
- Not caused by substance or medical condition

Specifiers: *with dissociative symptoms*, *with delayed expression* (full diagnostic criteria after at least 6 months from event)

Complex (C-PTSD) and continuous (CPTSD) posttraumatic stress disorder

C-PTSD: results more from chronic repetitive stress from which there is little chance of escape, for example, captivity. PTSD can result from a single event or short term exposure to extreme stress or trauma. It is this loss of a coherent sense of self and the ensuing symptom profile that most pointedly differentiates C-PTSD from PTSD (Herman, J. 1992).

CPTSD: term first used in 1987 in South Africa to describe the effects of exposure to political unrest and ongoing violence & civil conflict (Straker, G. 1987).

PTSD treatment issues.

- Potentially overwhelming emotion
- PTSD symptoms – spectrum (symptoms can vary in number and intensity)
- Atypical symptoms – visual hallucination

- Symptoms - intensity, frequency, duration
- Not psychotic, not "crazy"
- Coping strategy - discomfort is not danger
- Calming skills, grounding skills, etc.
- Healthy lifestyle skills
- Manage "triggers" – UCS/CS/CR
- The "2 and 2" for anxiety management
- Use of medication
- Treatment modalities
- C-PTSD, CPTSD, and traumatic grief
- Co-morbid substance use
- Other mental disorders
- Conception of mental injury as opposed to mental disorder
- Treatment considerations: individual support counseling, freezeframe processing, in the work setting or out, support network, peer support team, 24/7 contact support persons, formal group debriefing, resiliency

There are several stressor-related disorders and diagnoses in addition to PTSD (DSM-5). {briefly discuss the various stressor-related disorders}

- Brief psychotic disorder
- Conversion disorder
- Adjustment disorder
- Acute stress disorder
- Posttraumatic stress disorder
- Specified and unspecified trauma and stressor related disorders
- Various mood and anxiety disorders

Some clinical presentations do not seem to fit in any of the current diagnostic categories.

Primary symptoms of psychotic disorders {review primary psychotic symptoms – necessary because peer support team members must be able to recognize a brief psychotic disorder}

- hallucinations – disorder of perception (auditory most common but can involve all of the senses).
- delusions – disorder of thinking (tend to be persecutory or bizarre). Typical delusions are reference, influence, and thought insertion. Often, disturbing thoughts.
- emotional disturbance - often "negative" symptoms, impulse control issues, and emotional lability.
- loose associations - disorganized thinking, often reflected in disorganized speech (word salad).
- odd, unusual, or inappropriate behavior - inappropriate for context, bizarre speech, acting out, posturing, behavior consistent with responding to internal voices, etc.

Some PTSD and other disorder treatment modalities. {briefly discuss or review}

- Psychoanalysis
- Behavioral (reinforcement)
- Person-centered
- Cognitive-behavioral therapy
- Rational-emotive behavioral therapy
- Humanistic and existential
- Biofeedback
- EMDR
- Imagery rehearsal therapy
- Dialectical behavioral therapy
- Thought field therapy
- Hypnosis and altered states
- Time perspective therapy
- Exposure therapies – prolonged exposure, virtual exposure

Trauma intervention program (TIP). Sequence of support interventions for assisting officers involved in critical incidents - from on-scene support to return to duty and beyond (critical incident management) (Appendix F)

Precursor training – basic skills academy stress inoculation training and PATROL. Following critical incident:

- on-scene support – PST and others (important: contact from chief or sheriff)
- initiation into a counseling program
- assessment and appropriate intervention
- psychological visit to the incident location
- firing range and processing
- reintroduction to equipment
- TIP officer wellness assessment
- graded re-entry to duty
- appropriate follow-up

PST on scene support

- timely arrival
- initial contact – *do not touch involved officers* (although we might be inclined to shake hands, pat on the back, or hug those that have experienced a critical incident as a gesture of support, *do not touch an involved-officer in any manner* unless cleared to do so. (The officer, uniform, and police equipment may be evidence. Do not contaminate.)
- clarify PST role and limits of confidentiality
- remove involved officer from immediate area
- assess officer's status and well-being
- assist in meeting officer's immediate needs
- "walk and talk" if necessary and possible
- assist officer with variables which may be specific to incident *(not incident specifics!)*
- do not discuss the incident
- consideration: "Peer Support" identification (so as not to be assigned other duties or responsibilities – established in policy)
- follow your officer-involved incident protocol for peer support (if applicable)

PST scene coordination

- obtain available incident information from on scene supervisor – considerations?
- arrange for an adequate PST response (at possible multiple locations)
- assign PST members as necessary
- remember Dispatch and other pertinent personnel – deploy PST members
- as support unfolds, assess who needs *what* and *when*
- keep your PST coordinator informed
- make timely contact with your clinical supervisor
- request PST clinical supervisor to respond if part of protocol

FYI - There are on-scene assessments and interventions for severely traumatized persons that are beyond the scope of peer support. Contact your clinical supervisor immediately if you feel that someone has been severely traumatized.

Officer Wellness Assessment and Return-to-duty protocol.

- The Officer Wellness Assessment (OWA) is not a fitness-for-duty evaluation. The OWA is an assessment to determine (1) if the incident generated a stressor-related disorder that would prevent the officer from safely returning to duty, (2) if the incident exacerbated a pre-existing condition that would prevent the officer from safely returning to duty, and (3) the optimal timing for initiation of the return-to duty protocol (RTD).
- Sequence of events - the OWA is the last in a series of events which must take place prior to initiation of the return-to-duty protocol. Department policy determines whether an officer can be returned to duty before the officer is cleared by the DA's office and internal administrative investigation.
- The RTD is an individualized graded-reentry to duty – individualized for each officer - even if more than one officer is involved in the same incident. Many officers involved in

the same incident do not return to duty at the same time through the TIP. Graded reentry involves being accompanied by "buddy officers" in specified ways.

- Why graded reentry? Because prior assessment is insufficient to insure lack of difficulty returning to work. Graded reentry eases the officer's return to the environment within which the critical incident occurred. It also provides a support person (buddy officer) during the transition. {RTD's consisting of 35 hours have proven sufficient in most cases. To view an actual 35-hour RTD see *Reflections of a Police Psychologist* (2nd ed), page 94. Past RTDs have ranged from 15 hours to several weeks}
- Support continues for at least one year (psychologist and peer support) - "year of firsts" - first Christmas since the incident, first birthday since the incident, etc. Officer selects a peer support team member for a year of periodic check-in.

Law Enforcement Critical Incident Handbook

Present information about the Law Enforcement Critical Incident Handbook - available without cost from www.jackdigliani.com {PST members can download the Handbook at their convenience and make it available to incident-involved officers – some agencies distribute the Handbook to new officers during the basic in-service skills academy}

Included in the Law Enforcement Critical Incident Handbook: *Suggestions for Supporting Officers Involved in Shootings and Other Trauma* (Appendix G) and *25 Suggestions and Considerations For Officers Involved in a Critical Incident* (Appendix H) {briefly review the Suggestions and 25 Considerations – these are practical PST member guidelines for peer support and intervention – remain mindful of time restrictions}

Goal of peer support and other support interventions – positive survivor - stronger and smarter - placing the incident into psychological history. The goal of peer support and other support interventions following a critical incident is to have involved officers become positive survivors, to become *stronger and smarter.* The alternative is unacceptable (after surviving a critical incident, would "weaker and dumber" suffice?). Many officers become positive survivors and stronger and smarter following a critical incident. They know they did their best, learn from the experience, gain a new confidence, and place the incident into psychological history. A British police officer expressed this feature of positive survivorship this way...years after he defended a hostage by shooting and killing the suspect:

"...I am also aware how having come through both the incident and the aftermath, that I changed in a positive way too. I believe that dealing with the incident made me more resilient, able to cope better with problems and difficulties (based on a mind-set that goes something like "If I can deal with all of that, I can deal with anything that life throws at me"). The incident also reinforced my personal levels of professionalism (and my expectations of it in others). Over time these positives have, I believe, come to the fore, whilst the negative reactions have faded." (May 19, 2015)

Key points: history of trauma conception, critical incidents, perceptual distortions, common reactions during and following a critical incident, factors affecting magnitude of response, critical incident-traumatic incident, PTS and PTSD, treatment issues, Trauma Intervention Program, Law Enforcement Critical Incident Handbook, positive survivorship, stronger and smarter, positive outcomes.

Training objective: provide information related to critical and traumatic incidents; prepare class participants for critical incident peer support.

10. Concepts in critical incident exposure

Shock, impact, and recovery

Shock Phase: Various responses and reactions are possible in the shock phase. *Impact Phase*: Various thoughts and feelings characterize the impact phase. *Recovery Phase*: That period following the impact phase wherein the experience is slowly integrated into the person's life. For recovery: *You must find something positive in the experience* (at minimum, you survived) {describe possible responses and characteristics of each phase}

Concepts to consider and useful perspectives in police peer support

- The idea of 2nd injury
- Vicarious or "secondary" trauma
- Splitting of environments
- Fear vs helplessness vs vulnerability
- Role of reinforcement/conditioning
- Second-guessing paradigm - *X1 - time/more information -* X2 (decision made at X1 but later self-evaluated after more timer and information from X2 perspective). When helping a person consistently second guessing - "What would you say to a friend in similar circumstances?"

Second injury - also known as secondary injury - is the harm that can be caused to officers when they are poorly treated following involvement in a critical incident.

- The way an officer is treated following a critical incident such as a shooting is not benign.
- One way to virtually insure second injury following a police critical incident is to treat the involved officers as suspects.
- The smallest and seemingly innocuous insensitive statements, comments, or even thoughtless non-verbal glances or gestures may cause or contribute to an officer's second injury…but you don't have to walk on eggshells. Be professional – be yourself.

To avoid second injury: peers, investigators, supervisors, and command staff must keep in mind that the officers…

1. may have just survived a fight for their lives
2. may have had to use lethal force to protect another

3. may be variously impacted by various aspects of the incident
4. may be experiencing psychological denial and shock
5. may be experiencing reactions not easily observed by others
6. may have been physically injured

...and act accordingly. According to what? According to policy and procedure, trauma intervention programs, involved-officer protocols, peer support guidelines, basic functional and compassionate human interaction practices, etc.

Secondary trauma — also known as vicarious trauma — refers to the indirect traumatization that can occur when a person is exposed to others who have been directly traumatized. Secondary trauma is a real concern for the spouses and family members of officers that have been involved in a critical incident, as well as previously non-traumatized officers and others participating in agency critical incident debriefings.

Good to know:

- Everyone has a private life and some ability to look one way and feel another.
- Possible choices and decisions can lead to many possible consequences. Kurt Lewin: Human conflicts: approach-avoidance, approach-approach, avoidance-avoidance, and double approach-avoidance (1943, 1997).
- What to do? Tell me what to do...What should I do...What's the right thing to do...What would you do... (Is there really one right thing to do? There are several people in our lives who would be willing to tell us what to do. How helpful has it been?).
- Most often, life involves selecting from imperfect options.
- Some life circumstances cannot be improved or escaped emotionally unscathed.
- Think and feel through issues.
- Tunnel thinking & tunnel feeling (see chapter 4). State of mind can drive behavior.

- You can't always get what you want.
- There are things you can learn that no one can teach. Can follow traumatic exposure.
- Some things won't stop until you stop them. Some things won't start until you start them. Some things won't change until you change them.
- Life space, macro, and micro environments.
- Responsibility absorption. Responsibility absorption can be a theme in a person's life.
- "Red flags". Many flags are not red until you evaluate them from some future perspective. Are there "reds flags" that can be observed in the present and be used to construct an action plan? (yes) {discuss}
- You cannot not do your job. Implications for burnout, boreout, boundaries, career development, and your mental health. {provide examples}
- The other guy. It's not always the other guy, sometimes it's you. And even when it is the other guy, it's not the other guy to the other guy!
- Some things can be completely or partially controlled. Some things cannot be controlled. It is better to focus on things that can be controlled, which includes your response to things that cannot be controlled. Some things that cannot be controlled can be influenced. In reference to long held ideas or interaction patterns: "Do you control it, or does it control you?" "How long will you let it control you?" What are we talking about? {initiate class discussion}

Anger. Everyone gets mad sometimes, but how does anger relate to stress and trauma?

- Chronic anger vs. situational anger vs. stress or trauma generated anger
- Anger as the only emotion to penetrate the defense mechanism *emotional insulation*
- Anger as more acceptable for some persons than other emotions (like feeling hurt)

- Anger as a learned response, reinforced by results.
- Consequences of anger {discuss common consequences of anger and angry acting out}

Personal Boundary. A personal boundary is an understanding that there is only so much you can do for another person. This is why there is an emphasis in peer support on empowering others. You must maintain a reasonable personal boundary when providing peer support so that the person's problems do not become your problems. You compromise your personal boundary at the risk of your psychological and physical well-being. Considerations:

1. Limit of how responsible one person can be for another person
2. Limit of what one person can do for another person
3. The border where one person "ends" and another person "begins"
4. Supporting independence vs. fostering dependence
5. Focus on empowerment
6. Related to secondary trauma and personal well-being
7. Personal boundaries are critical for support team members

Peer support issues and strategies. {some have been presented previously but they are worth repeating (cognitive reinforcement). Especially important strategies are in bold type}

- **walk and talk** to dissipate the stress response after a critical incident
- **surface lesson/deep lesson** - the surface lesson is the more obvious conclusion to be generated by some experience, while the deep lesson is the deeper meaning personally attached to the experience. The deep lesson is often irrational, tends create anxiety, and can cause life difficulties. Example: "My ex cheated on me, he cannot be trusted (rational surface lesson). No one is trustworthy" (irrational deep lesson)

- **options vs. threat funnel** (as police officer options for interaction diminish, the personal threat level to the officer increases – at the bottom of the option funnel lies self-defense)
- **the 2 and 2** - "I know what this is, I know what to do about it" and "stronger and smarter"
- survivorship vs. victimization
- stay grounded in what you know to be true (use strategy to help buffer officers against unfair or untrue criticism)
- having the right vs. is it right (legal vs moral – a conflict sometimes observed in officers following a work-related shooting. Can occur even in circumstances where the officer would likely have been killed had not lethal force been used in defense)
- selecting from imperfect options
- I'm in trouble vs. I'm alive
- **intervention as the 2nd best option** (time machine = the best option). "With a time machine we could go back with what we now know and prevent a critical or undesirable incident. Being that the best option is not available, we must work together to do the best we can to move forward." (this simple cognitive presentation often helps officers to diminish the wishful thinking that is sometimes present following a critical incident. It helps officers move past wishing that the incident did not happen. It helps officers to focus on the "here and now" and eventual recovery
- police authority in America is intentionally limited
- American society accepts a margin of risk for law enforcement officers, as do officers themselves

Internal investigations and the peer support team.

Officers involved in critical incidents such as an officer-involved shooting, will become involved in two types of investigations: criminal (right to remain silent) (Miranda v. Arizona, 1966) and administrative (no right to remain silent) (Garrity v. New Jersey, 1967) {briefly discuss these types of investigations and how they relate to each other – flow of information} Several departments now include a psychologist and peer support statement within the document that advises officers they are the subject of an administrative (internal) investigation: "you may contact the department psychologist or any uninvolved member of the peer support team."

Key points: shock-impact-recovery, second injury, secondary trauma, second guessing, selecting from imperfect options, tunnel thinking and feeling, micro environments, not always the other guy, anger, personal boundaries, red flags, walk and talk, surface lesson/deep lesson, options vs. threat funnel, the 2 and 2, time machine, risk for police officers, types of investigations.

Training objective: acquaint class participants with issues and strategies involved in critical incident exposure and critical incident peer support.

11. Peer support team confidentiality

Comprehensive presentation and discussion of PST statutory confidentiality protections (if applicable), department PST policy, and PST operational guidelines. In Colorado, C.R.S. 13-90-107 (m). {importance of this core topic is emphasized}

PST limits of confidentiality

How important is it for PST members to specify the limits of peer support team member confidentiality? (*extremely important* – recipients of peer support must be advised of the conditions under which PST-interaction information might be or must be disclosed before engaging in peer support) Unless advised of confidentiality limitations, recipients of peer support may falsely believe that all information discussed in peer support interactions is confidential. {the development of peer support "limits of confidentiality" pocket cards is encouraged – if you have them, distribute to class participants. Pocket cards may be read and provided to those seeking peer support – see Appendix I}

If PST members find advising awkward, consider something like this, "I want to do the best I can for you – let's take a minute to talk about peer support team member confidentiality…" Use the pocket card if needed.

What if the person decides not to engage peer support after PST confidentiality limits are discussed? (PST members support them to seek other and possibly more confidential resources. If warranted, assess for suicidality and other-person safety)

Good to know: information discussed within peer support interactions may be disclosed by recipients of peer support. *A recipient of peer support does not need your permission to talk about your peer support interaction.* This means that the person can disclose any or all information discussed, including what you did and what you said without your consent. Bottom line: stay professional.

PST members, critical incident-involved officers, and attorneys

PST members should avoid being present when an involved officer is discussing a critical incident with his or her attorney. Why? Because even in states which provide some statutory confidentiality protections for PST members, there is currently no similar protection in the federal court system. Also, in some states, the attorney-client confidentiality privilege may not extend to third parties, or it may be compromised in the presence of a non-client third party. Best and safest option – do not become involved in officer-attorney discussions.

- What if the officer insists you remain? (advise the officer of your confidentiality limitations and that you will remain close by – return when attorney consultation is completed)

PST waiver of confidentiality

- How does a person waive confidentiality? (by signing or providing a confidentiality waiver)

- What is your responsibility when a person you have been providing peer support waives his/her peer support privilege of confidentiality? (discuss pertinent information with those identified in the waiver if requested)
- Should confidentiality waivers be in writing? (yes, but there is a common practice for verbal waivers in everyday peer support interactions – personal judgment is imperative here. If there is any doubt, obtain a written waiver)
- Where do I get an *"Authorization for the Release of Information"* form? (Police and Sheriff Peer Support Team Manual)

Duty to warn. Refers to the responsibility of clinicians to inform authorities and others if a client poses a threat to identified individuals. Advising authorities is insufficient. Persons that have been threatened must also be notified. Legally established in the case of Tarasoff v. Regents of the University of California (1976). Police were notified of threats but this notification was determined to be insufficient. Tatiana Tarasoff was subsequently murdered by Prosenjit Poddar. Extended in Jablonski by Pahls v. United States (1983) for cases involving risk assessment (must review historical records). Melinda Kimball was murdered by the man she was living with, Phillip Jablonski. {discuss duty-to-warn issues, police officer involvement and police action, and expectations for members of police peer support teams}

Criminal confessions and information. Information pertaining to criminal activity is not protected in states that currently have a police peer support team member confidentiality statute.

1. In the event that a person begins to communicate "information indicative of any criminal conduct" (from: Colorado Revised Statutes 13-90-107m), immediately stop the peer support discussion *in this area*. Do not stop peer support.
2. Remind the person that such information is not protected and it's best to stop this area of discussion. (you should

have already mentioned this in your "limits of confidentiality" disclosure prior to engaging in peer support)

3. If the person insists on talking to you about criminal activity (self-involved or otherwise) after a reminder of non-confidentiality, it may be that he intends to report this information to you or the police department and is requesting your support. Clarify his intentions. Provide peer support as requested.

4. *Do not leave the person alone,* especially if a police officer.

5. Contact your clinical supervisor *immediately.* Together, devise a plan of action, which may include contacting a department investigator. Stay with the person and continue peer support until otherwise directed by your clinical supervisor.

6. Some circumstances must be reported. Some circumstances require that other action be taken. In some circumstances, some discretion is possible depending upon the kind of information presented and statutory requirements. What are some examples of these cases? {discuss examples – avoid making examples unreasonably complex}

7. Peer support team members are committed to helping others, however *police peer support team members are not required to, and do not jeopardize themselves professionally or ethically by concealing ongoing or past criminal activity.*

<u>Important</u>: Stopping a peer support conversation when a person begins to discuss information indicative of any criminal conduct is not an effort to assist the person to conceal or cover-up past or ongoing criminal behavior. Quite the contrary, peer support interactions encourage honesty and the assumption of personal responsibility. Instead, stopping the conversation and following up as indicated recognizes the fact that you can better assist the person if you are not placed in a position where you might become a witness in a possible prosecution. As it is, you may be required to take action and/or testify based upon the information already presented.

If a person that has been advised of the limits of peer support team confidentiality insists on talking to you about information that is not protected, you must act upon the information as you would if you were not a member of the peer support team. This is especially true for sworn police officer members of the peer support team.

If you have any concerns or questions about any information provided to you in a peer support interaction, contact your clinical supervisor immediately. You do not have to interpret or sort out ambiguous peer support confidentiality circumstances on your own.

Key points: confidentiality statute, policy, organizational guidelines, limits of confidentiality, confidentiality waivers, recipients do not need your consent to discuss peer support interactions. duty-to-warn, officer-attorney discussions, criminal activity information and peer support.

Training objective: comprehension of peer support team confidentiality standards and the complexity of particular peer support interactions.

12. Confidentiality, clinical supervision, and oversight

Supervisor/advisor- PST member confidentiality. The PST Supervisor/ Advisor and peer support team member "confidentiality highway" is a one way street. As specified in policy and/or organizational guidelines, information can move from PST member to clinical supervisor without a waiver. However, information provided to the clinical supervisor by a person in a counseling setting cannot move to a PST member without a waiver. This is because the counseling relationship between psychologist and client is independent of peer support. {this one-way arrangement is necessary to provide clinical oversight of peer support interactions while providing confidentiality in the professional counseling setting. The fact that peer support information will be shared with the PST clinical supervisor must be included in the peer support "limits of confidentiality" disclosure}

Definition of "bring under supervision." To bring a peer support interaction under supervision is to inform your clinical supervisor (or advisor) of whom you are working with and the primary issues you are addressing (clinical supervisors, in some peer support interactions, may not require the identity of the peer support recipient). Your supervisor may ask questions or make recommendations for your peer support interactions so that the quality of your peer support is enhanced.

Bringing your peer support interactions under supervision. Some peer support interactions must be brought under supervision immediately (like suicidal ideation and criminal activity information). Some clinical supervision can take place in the group setting (usually involving reach-outs, information that is already public or department-wide knowledge, waived confidentiality for the PST, etc). Some information discussed within peer support interactions should be brought under supervision privately (information pertaining to medical conditions and personal relationships are good examples of what should be brought under supervision privately, unless there is expressed consent to share the information with other members of the peer support team). General rule - if you have any doubt about whether supervision should be done in the group setting or privately, *do it privately.*

PST member confidentiality issues – summary and review.

- Unless you have a waiver of confidentiality, you cannot talk to other peer support team members, including the PST coordinator, about specific peer support interactions. *Persons that seek peer support do not automatically consent to having their information shared with other members of the peer support team.*
- In the real world, peer support confidentiality waivers often consist of a casual verbal statement, something like "you can talk to Victor (another PST member) about this. I have already spoken to him about it." In such cases, a formal written waiver of confidentiality is seldom completed. However, if the issue is serious or likely to result in a court proceeding, a written confidentiality waiver should be obtained.

- Remember, when provided for in PST policy or operational guidelines, you do not need a waiver to talk to your clinical supervisor, but this must be disclosed in your "limits of confidentiality" prior to engaging in peer support.
- Peer support team members can seek peer support from other peer support team members about issues in their own lives. In such cases, all the responsibilities of peer support team members and all of the confidentiality protections provided to recipients of peer support apply.

Class activity. Peer support team member presentation: selected experienced PST member(s) present actual *types* of cases (not actual cases) that have involved members of the peer support team. Also discussed are (1) peer support strategies, (2) how clinical supervision was utilized, and (3) general outcomes, if known. Then, question and answer period.

Referral to professional services. When to refer? {discuss circumstances that indicate referral is desirable or necessary} (issues beyond peer support, suicidal ideation, troubled previous history with an officer seeking peer support, degradation of an existing peer support relationship, etc)

Referral resources. (Who can you refer to?)

- other peer support team members
- clinical supervisor
- employee assistance program (most EAPs include financial and legal assistance)
- community mental health professionals
- medical professionals
- legal professionals
- clergy and department chaplain (if applicable)
- military veteran services (VA, etc)
- any other appropriate and available support persons or organizations.

Referral does not mean peer support needs to stop. Peer support may continue in conjunction with the engagement of referral support or counseling resources.

PST member helpful information:

Stay in contact with your clinical supervisor.

Stay in compliance with the clinical supervision provisions of your operational guidelines.

If a peer support interaction is not under clinical supervision as outlined in your guidelines and training, it is not Level II peer support. Therefore, (in Colorado) that particular interaction would not be protected under department policy or C.R.S. 13-90-107(m). Why? (because your interaction is not in compliance with the department's written guidelines – written guidelines as required by Colorado statute)

Key points: relationship of clinical supervisor and PST members, one-way information highway, supervision and oversight, class activity, referral.

Training objective: further develop the understanding of PST confidentiality and its relationship to clinical supervision and oversight; identify factors involved in referral.

13. Foundations of peer support and intervention strategies

Brief review of the major schools of psychology: psychoanalysis, behaviorism, cognitive-behavioral, and humanistic-existential {presented to provide class participants with a brief history of psychological conceptualization and intervention theory}

Psychoanalysis: id-ego-superego, brief discussion of developmental theory and perspective of pathology (Freud)

Behaviorism: learning and reinforcement theory, brief discussion of primary principles (Pavlov and Skinner)

- Classical conditioning – UCS/UCR, CS/CR
- Positive reinforcement - the presentation of a reward. The reward increases the probability that the behavior which occurred just prior to the reward will be repeated. Thus, that particular behavior is strengthened (reinforced).
- Negative reinforcement – the termination of an unpleasant stimulus upon the performance of some behavior. The behavior which is associated with the cessation of the unpleasant stimulus is thereby strengthened and likely to be repeated (not to be confused with punishment).
- Punishment - is not a reinforcer because it does not strengthen a response or behavior. Punishment is the presentation of an unpleasant stimulus and tends to suppress and decrease the probability of the behavior which occurred just prior to its presentation. Punishment does not provide information about more acceptable alternatives. Punishment also often elicits emotional reactions such as anger or fear. Normally, the more severe the punishment, the more intense the reaction. Positive punishment: presentation of an unpleasant stimulus (spanking). Negative punishment: removal of a desired object or circumstance (taking away a favorite toy).
- Shaping - the rewarding of successive approximations to the desired behavior.
- Extinction - the cessation of a behavior following the cessation of reward.

Schedules of reinforcement

- Continuous reinforcement - the reinforcement of a response each time it occurs. Works best when first learning something new. Produces the fastest learning.
- Partial reinforcement - the intermittent reinforcement of a response. Intermittent reinforcement may occurs in several ways:

1. Fixed ratio schedule: reinforces a response after it occurs a set number of times ($5.00 for every 10 items made - piecework method of compensation).
2. Variable ratio schedule: reinforces a response after it occurs varying number of times (slot machine). Most resistant to extinction.
3. Fixed interval schedule: reinforces responses after a set period of time (paycheck every two weeks).
4. Variable interval schedule: reinforces responses after varying periods of time (some contract arrangements).

- Primary reinforcers - involve rewards that aid biological survival (food, water, sleep, etc.)
- Secondary reinforcers – rewards that strengthen responses which do not aid biological survival (verbal praise, non-verbal winks, nods, thumbs up, etc.) {discuss how these principles might be observed and be applied in peer support}

Cognitive-behavioral: discussion of cognitive-behavioral theory/ therapy.

Cognitive-behavioral therapy (CBT) is based on the idea that thoughts create and cause our feelings and drive our behavior…not external things, like people, situations, and events. The benefit of this perspective is that we can change the way we think so that we feel and act differently even if the situation does not change (From: National Association of Cognitive-Behavioral Therapists)

Varied and broad application of CBT.

- Cognitive mediation - *influencing or controlling one part of the brain with another part of the brain* (most often – influencing or controlling undesired emotional responses with thinking-coping strategies)
- To the degree that this can be accomplished, dysfunctional thoughts and behavior can be mitigated
- CBT is a useful perspective in peer support

<u>Humanistic-existential</u>: person-centered and existence perspective (Rogers)

"This process of the good life is not, I am convinced, a life for the faint-hearted. It involves the stretching and growing, of becoming more and more of one's potentialities. It involves the courage to be. It means launching oneself fully into the stream of life." (Rogers, C. 1961).

Rogers regarded every one as a "potentially competent individual" who could benefit greatly from his form of therapy. The purpose of Roger's humanistic therapy is to increase a person's feelings of self-worth, reduce the level of incongruence between the ideal and actual self, and help a person become more of a fully functioning person. Person-centered therapy operates according to three basic principles that reflect the attitude of the therapist to the person:

- The therapist is congruent with the person.
- The therapist provides the [erson with unconditional positive regard.
- The therapist shows empathetic understanding to the person. (McLeod, S. A., 2008.) {discuss these principles in easily understandable terms)

Existential – issues of existence. {briefly discuss historical and current existential perspectives}

<u>Key points</u>: psychoanalysis, behaviorism, schedules of reinforcement, cognitive-behavioral therapy, influencing one part of the brain with another part of the brain, humanistic-existential perspectives.

<u>Training objective</u>: provide foundation information pertaining to counseling theory and helping perspectives; build foundation for concepts utilized in peer support.

14. Model for peer support

Police peer support: Three stage model (Egan, G., 2006)

- Stage I   *Exploration*
- Stage II *Person Objective Understanding*
- Stage III *Action Programs*

Stage I: Exploration

1. Attending	7. Transparency
2. Effective (active) listening	8. Reflection
3. Genuineness	9. Respect
4. Empathy	10. Trust
5. Concreteness	11. Summary
6. Non-judgmental	12. Assessment

{explain and discuss each of the components of Stage I}

Counseling continuum: directive /non-directive {explain difference, pros and cons of each}

Good to know:

- People do not change easily.
- Dysfunctional behavior is frequently reinforced in some way...it serves some need or purpose.
- Habitual dysfunctional behaviors lead to dysfunctional behavioral patterns.
- Meet the need being served by a dysfunctional pattern in a more functional way and the dysfunctional pattern will diminish.
- To help initiate and maintain desired change...talk to yourself. Talk to yourself in a way that those supporting your efforts would talk to you. Use self-talk to alter behavior for yourself and to help others.

<u>Stage II</u>: Person objective understanding (finding new perspectives)

1. Self-disclosure
2. Confrontation
3. Advanced accurate empathy
4. Immediacy

(1) Self-disclosure - involves sharing your thoughts, feelings, experiences, and reactions. Normally increases intimacy or "depth" of relationship. Can normalize the person's experiences or feelings. Can encourage the person to talk more about previously avoided topics. Can change the person's opinion of you. Share only what is comfortable for you. Can be overdone – do not make it about you. Avoid "enabling" through self-disclosure. *Do not make the person seeking peer support your therapist.*

(2) Confrontation – (for peer support) do not confront another person if you do not intend to increase your involvement. Confront only if you experience feelings of caring or some sense of connection. Avoid confronting when angry. Confront only if the relationship has gone beyond the initial stages of development or if basic trust has been clearly established.

*   If the conditions above are present and the person is not ready to deal with the information non-defensively, then you have two basic options: avoid confrontation or help the person become ready to use the information once it is presented.

How to confront constructively

*   Present the data on which the inferences are based before stating the inference.
*   Distinguish between observations and inferences and make that distinction verbally clear in the message to the person.
*   State inferences tentatively.
*   Use "I messages" throughout the confrontation.

(3) Advanced accurate empathy - advanced accurate empathy goes beyond another's verbal and non-verbal expressions. When accurate, it represents a deeper understanding, a degree of insight, and a summation of what another person is thinking and feeling. What happens if your empathy is inaccurate? (most persons will correct you – accept their feedback and continue peer support)

(4) Immediacy - what's happening now. Immediacy involves moving the focus of the discussion from whatever is being presented to what is happening right now (immediately) between you and the other person.

Stage III - Action programs.

Characteristics of good action programs:

1. Concrete workable goals
2. Set priorities
3. Check behaviors
4. Make it effective
5. Move from less serious to more serious when possible
6. Consider the person's values
7. Develop relapse-prevention strategies
8. Appropriate follow-up

Peer support team 10-Step CBT-based action program:

Step 1: Have I clearly identified the problem.
Step 2: How am I thinking about the problem?
Step 3: Are my thoughts rational or irrational? (seek help if you do not know)
Step 4: Is there a better way to re-think or conceptualize the problem?
Step 5: What do I wish to change?
Step 6: What behaviors do I wish to change?
Step 7: What are the possible obstacles to my desired changes?
Step 8: How will I overcome these obstacles?

Step 9: How and when will I implement my plan?
Step 10: How will I evaluate the outcome and maintain positive
    change? How will I prevent a relapse to dysfunction?

Action plans are most helpful when they are written. To improve
the effectiveness of an action plan you can provide the person
with a copy of the *Peer Support Team Action Plan Worksheet.* The
person can also design a personal action plan. Action plans may
be used in conjunction with peer support or may be independent
of peer support. {the Peer Support Team Action Plan Worksheet
is included in Police and Sheriff Peer Support Team Manual}

Supporting positive change in peer support: Support the person to
make a positive change even if it seems small -

- Psychological change
- Cognitive change
- Emotional change
- Behavior change

Sometimes changing a behavior is easier than changing anything
else. Even small, accomplished changes in behavior can motivate a
person to continue effort. Changing behavior is a great place to start.

Good to know – information and summary

- a common mistake in peer support is trying to move from
    Stage I to Stage III too fast - in fact, you can consistently
    support a person by remaining in Stage I, Exploration
- avoid imposing your world view
- remain within the parameters of the PST program and your
    training
- contact your team coordinator or clinical supervisor if
    questions arise
- peer support team members have a commitment to enhance
    the independence of those they are supporting – avoid
    fostering dependency

- use care if working with people you dislike - refer to other PST members if you cannot remain professional (much depends on how much dislike there is – a peer support team member should not begin peer support with a person for whom there exists a great deal of animosity)
- if *you* have unfinished psychological or emotional business, seek appropriate support or counseling
- do not become the client of the person you are trying to help
- in the words of the 1960's, *"Don't lay your trip on the person you're trying to help"*

Peer support information:

- *Blinded by the principle* (cognitive rigidity that drives dysfunctional behavior) Example: "Real men win every argument"
- Seeing things from other perspectives is a skill to be learned
- Seeing things from another's perspective, also a skill to be learned
- Working within another's thought and value system

Peer support skills: reflective listening, paraphrasing, and summarization {define and discuss these peer support skills}

Video presentation: reflective listening, paraphrasing, and summarization (Richardson, D., 2010) {use to demonstrate concepts, then discuss pros and cons of this particular presentation}

Discussion of the following and how they relate to peer support:

- "learned helplessness" as a component of depression (Navy – torture resistance) (Positive Psychology) (Martin Seligman)
- cognitive restructuring
- rational-emotive behavioral therapy (REBT) (Albert Ellis) A-B-C-D *adversity-belief-consequence-dispute.* REBT Basic Philosophies - unconditional self-acceptance USA,

unconditional other-acceptance UOA, unconditional life-acceptance ULA. The 12 REBT irrational ideas that cause and sustain neurosis (Appendix J). Ellis's most frequent advice — "deal with it"

Video presentation: Albert Ellis – on REBT {available on internet}

REBT irrational idea number 9 – "The idea that because something once strongly affected our life, it should indefinitely affect it - instead of the idea that we can learn from our past experiences but not be overly-attached to or prejudiced by them" (application for police critical incidents, PTS, and PTSD? What do you think? {class discussion}

Key points: stage model for peer support, action plan, supporting positive change, concepts in peer support, REBT.

Training objective: development of basic peer support skills by applying the stage model of counseling; familiarization with practical peer support concepts.

15. Peer support tips

Peer support tips – a summary collection of easily recalled practical factors and useful things to remember when providing peer support. As a summary, the peer support tips necessarily include some previously presented information: {excellent for reinforcement of appropriate peer support behaviors}

- Find a comfortable physical setting when possible
- Keep in mind that privacy may be very important for the person
- Clarify your PST role and specify PST limits of confidentiality
- Be mindful of timing and circumstances
- Develop a working alliance
- Engage appropriate humor when appropriate. Don't overdo it!
- Make it safe for communication

- Proceed slowly – it is not helpful to be perceived as "rushed"
- If you don't have time to meet when contacted, set a time to meet
- Listen closely – speak briefly
- Listen for metaphors that can be used in exploration - use similar metaphors when appropriate
- Do not assume that you know the persons feelings, thoughts, and behaviors
- Avoid interruptions and distractions (from *you* and the environment)
- Process information in a supportive manner – engage attentive body language, practice active listening, maintain a non-judgmental attitude, use reflective statements, paraphrase
- Help the person explore (Stage I support skill) but avoid relying *solely* on questions. Over-questioning can increase a person's defensiveness and decrease the effectiveness of peer support
- Do not move from Stage I *Exploration* to Stage III *Action Programs* too quickly
- Notice resistance – communicate to process alternatives
- Emphasize strengths – encourage empowerment
- When in doubt, focus on emotions and feelings – avoid saying "how does that make you feel?" - instead say something like "That must have been difficult. Tell me more about how that affected you"
- When you don't know what to say, say nothing or "Tell me more"
- Pay attention to nonverbal behaviors (*mind* yours and *notice* theirs)
- Agreement does not equal empathy – you do not need to agree with the views of a person to be empathetic
- Do not reinforce dysfunctional thoughts and behaviors
- Gently confront dysfunctional thoughts and behaviors
- Remember, if you confront too much too soon, the person will likely disengage from you and peer support

- Do not assume change is easy – identify and discuss obstacles to change
- Conduct a field assessment for suicidal thinking and behavior if warranted
- Summarize periodically and at the end of the support meeting
- Stay within the boundaries of your peer support training
- Set a future time to meet again if warranted
- Bring your interactions under clinical supervision
- Refer to available professional resources when appropriate (Meier, S.T. & Davis, S.R., 2011 and Digliani, J.A., 2015)

Video presentation – Counselling skills: knock three times (Barton, R., 2011). {available at http//www.youtube.com}

Peer Support: re-frame, re-interpret, re-conceptualize. Frame the problem so that there can be some resolution or improvement. Reframe prior unsuccessful efforts as contributing to "the value of experience." Establish a safety net. Can include a "ring down" list of persons to call if things get tough. Safety net is a concept in peer support and in the proactive PATROL and RTD programs.

Education: Officers must assume greater responsibility for their psychological health and learn to ask for help when feeling stressed or overwhelmed. {part of the upcoming Make it Safe Police Officer Initiative discussion}

New PST member assets: the biggest assets for new PST members are: (1) the PST Manual, (2) your clinical supervisor, and (3) experienced PST members.

New PST members should not be reluctant to engage in Level II peer support. Trust yourself and your training. When it comes to peer support, NIKE had it right: Just do it. Remember, *inexperience is not inability.*

Class activity - practical exercise role play: peer support with emphasis on Stage I (Exploration). "Create groups of three. Form a group with persons not well known to you (if possible). Each person will assume one of three roles - a PST member, a person seeking peer support, and an observer. Each person will eventually assume each role." {Each person spends 10-12 minutes in each role.} Some fictional scenarios for this activity are presented below:

- a supervisor that "plays favorites"
- an officer-spouse that is stressed by the hours of shift work
- a child that is misbehaving at school
- personal difficulty sleeping & feeling tired much of the time
- officer not sure of desire to continue in law enforcement
- civilian police department employee not feeling part of the "police family"

{fictional issues, even though they mimic real issues, are used because this is not the forum for processing actual issues. Once each person in each group has had the opportunity to assume each role, the activity is ended. Each group then discusses their experiences with the class and receives feedback from other class members. The trainer utilizes the information presented to advance knowledge, to provide feedback, and to reinforce positive participant skills. The trainer notes that role playing peer support is often more difficult than actual peer support. The activity and following discussion usually requires 60 to 90 minutes, depending upon the size of the class. Although many officers cringe at the idea of role-play, this activity has proven to be instructional, experiential, and a welcome change from lecture. The trainer should endeavor to make this exercise non-threatening, educational, and even fun}

Key points: peer support tips, peer support role-play, discussion of role-play experience.

Training objective: provide practical "how to" peer support information; experience brief Level II peer support role-play.

16. Alcohol, drugs, and addictions

- Neurobiological perspective: addiction as a disease of the reward centers of the brain
- Most experts agree that although drug abuse begins as a voluntary behavior, at some point a critical point is crossed and it becomes a brain disease
- Each drug manipulates the reward circuitry in a bit different way, but all substances of abuse activate the same pleasure pathway in the brain
- Pleasure pathway: *nucleus accumbens*, the "universal site of addiction" (including nicotine and alcohol)
- The brain is tricked into acting as if it needs the substance to survive
- These substances change the molecular structure of the brain
- In experiments, rats will press a lever for cocaine until it kills them

Substance information:

- alcohol: *dose dependent* - many effects in the brain (behavioral disinhibitor to toxic)
- natural "opiates": naturally present in the brain. Serve to lift mood, motivate behavior, moderate pain. Opium based drugs are much more potent than naturally occurring brain chemicals
- methamphetamine - creates a "dopamine dump"
- cocaine – stimulant, appetite suppressant, triple reuptake inhibitor (dopamine, serotonin, norepinephrine), some medical uses, second most abused drug in US (behind MJ)
- marijuana - active ingredient - THC (delta-9-tetrahydrocannabinol), most commonly abused illicit drug in the United States. Medical MJ? Recreational MJ? Both now legal in some states
- caffeine, nicotine, sex, food? Can you become addicted? What are "process" addictions? {discuss known facts and various views}

Substance use disorders – example: alcohol use disorder - DSM-5

A. A problematic pattern of alcohol use leading to clinically significant impairment or distress.

B. Two (or more) of the following occurring within a 12-month period:

1. Alcohol is often taken in larger amounts or over a longer period than was intended
2. There is a persistent desire or unsuccessful effort to cut down or control alcohol use
3. A great deal of time is spent in activities necessary to obtain alcohol, use the substance, or recover from its effects
4. Recurrent alcohol use resulting in a failure to fulfill major role obligations at work, school, or home (e.g., repeated absences or poor work performance related to alcohol use; substance-related absences, suspensions, or expulsions from school; neglect of children or household)
5. Continued alcohol use despite having persistent or recurrent social or interpersonal problems caused or exacerbated by the effects of the substance
6. Important social, occupational, or recreational activities are given up or reduced because of alcohol use
7. Recurrent alcohol use in situations in which it is physically hazardous (e.g., driving an automobile or operating a machine when impaired by substance use
8. Alcohol use is continued despite knowledge of having a persistent or recurrent physical or psychological problem that is likely to have been caused or exacerbated by the substance
9. Tolerance, as defined by either or both of the following:

   a. A need for markedly increased amounts of alcohol to achieve intoxication or desired effect
   b. Markedly diminished effect with continued use of the same amount of the substance

10. Withdrawal, as manifested by either of the following:

    a.   The characteristic withdrawal syndrome for alcohol (refer to Criteria A and B of the criteria set for Withdrawal)

    b.   The same (or a closely related) substance is taken to relieve or avoid withdrawal symptoms

11. Craving or a strong desire or urge to use alcohol {extrapolate to other substance use disorders}

25 warning signs of alcoholism

1. Do you ever drink after telling yourself you won't?
2. Does your drinking worry your family?
3. Have you ever been told that you drink too much?
4. Do you drink alone when you feel angry or sad?
5. Have you ever felt you should cut down on your drinking?
6. Do you get headaches or have hangovers after drinking?
7. Has your drinking ever make you late for work?
8. Have you ever been arrested because of your drinking?
9. Have people annoyed you by criticizing your drinking?
10. Have you ever felt bad or guilty about your drinking?
11. Have you ever substituted drinking for a meal?
12. Have you tried to stop drinking or to drink less and failed?
13. Have you ever felt embarrassed or remorseful about your behavior due to drinking?
14. Do you drink secretly to avoid the concerns or criticisms of others?
15. Do you ever forget what you did while you were drinking?
16. Stockpiling alcohol.
17. Hiding alcohol.
18. Planning your activities to insure that alcohol is available.
19. For women - Have you continued drinking while pregnant? (even small amounts)
20. For women - Have you continued drinking while breastfeeding? (even if only between feedings or in small amounts)

21. Have you ever had a drink first thing in the morning to steady your nerves or get rid of a hangover?
22. Have you ever had to take a drink while at work to feel better?
23. Do you feel shaky, unsettled, or sick if you do not have a drink for a few days?
24. Do you look for occasions to justify drinking?
25. Alcohol becomes number one in your life.

Alcoholism: disease or choice? Perspectives: (1) Substance addiction is a complex but treatable brain disease. It is characterized by compulsive drug craving, drug seeking, and use that persist even in the face of severe adverse consequences. (2) Substance addiction is not a disease, but a choice in lifestyle. {briefly discuss}

Alcoholism and the ADA: briefly discuss the alcohol addiction provisions of the Americans with Disabilities Act as it relates to protection of employment when an employee seeks voluntary treatment. {at minimum, PST members should be able to provide basic information about alcohol and other substance use. They must be able to appropriately refer a person who comes to them for help with an alcohol or other substance use or addiction concern}

Some treatment programs

- residential & non-residential programs
- counseling and psychotherapy (individual and group)
- lifestyle counseling and life skills
- CBT – "think about what you're thinking"
- AA, NA, GA and other 12-step programs
- Non-12 step programs (SMART, CRAFT, etc)

The 12 steps of Alcoholics Anonymous (AA) {many officers have heard of 12-step programs but are unfamiliar with the actual steps – most 12-step programs are spiritually based. Regardless of a trainer's personal views, class participants should be familiar with these steps and some non-12 step programs – may be slight variations in 12-step text from various sources}

1. We admitted we were powerless over alcohol - that our lives had become unmanageable.
2. Came to believe that a Power greater than ourselves could restore us to sanity.
3. Made a decision to turn our will and our lives over to the care of God as we understood Him.
4. Made a searching and fearless moral inventory of ourselves.
5. Admitted to God, to ourselves, and to another human being the exact nature of our wrongs.
6. Were entirely ready to have God remove all these defects of character.
7. Humbly asked Him to remove our shortcomings.
8. Made a list of all persons we had harmed, and became willing to make amends to them all.
9. Made direct amends to such people wherever possible, except when to do so would injure them or others.
10. Continued to take personal inventory and when we were wrong promptly admitted it.
11. Sought through prayer and meditation to improve our conscious contact with God as we understood Him, praying only for knowledge of His will for us and the power to carry that out.
12. Having had a spiritual awakening as a result of these steps, we tried to carry this message to alcoholics, and to practice these principles in all our affairs.

Success and AA. "...figures compiled by Alcoholics Anonymous, probably the world's most high-profile treatment program, reveal that 64% of their members drop out in the first year. They also reveal that 84% of AA members do not exclusively rely on the AA's *12-Step Program* promoted in its group sessions, but supplement this with outside help from various sources. In fact, 31% of AA members have been referred to AA by other treatment centers. The many people who have been cured of their alcohol addiction through AA tend to be zealous in their support for the organization, but this cannot mask the fact that, for most people, it has not worked." (Retrieved 2015 from: http://alcoholrehab.com) {discuss support and criticism of AA and 12-step models, and the apparently poor success rates for substance addiction treatment generally}

Substance treatment.

Traditional concepts: "intervention", "confrontation", "rock bottom", "enabling", "one drink away" "disease" etc.

CRAFT – *Community Reinforcement and Family Training*

- Non-confrontive
- Positive reinforcement, positive alternatives
- Role playing & training for family members

Natural consequences (Retrieved 2015 from http://www.robertjmeyersphd.com)

SMART - *Self Management for Addiction Recovery*

- Teaches self-empowerment and self-reliance.
- Provides meetings that are educational, supportive and include open discussions.
- Encourages individuals to recover from addiction and alcohol abuse and live satisfying lives.
- Teaches techniques for self-directed change.
- Supports the scientifically informed use of psychological treatments and legally prescribed psychiatric and addiction medication.
- Works on substance abuse, alcohol abuse, addiction and drug abuse as complex maladaptive behaviors with possible physiological factors.
- Evolves as scientific knowledge in addiction recovery evolves.
- Differs from Alcoholics Anonymous, Narcotics Anonymous and other 12-step programs. (Retrieved 2015 from http://www.smartrecovery.org)

Motivated interview: *Four General Principles* - express empathy, develop discrepancy, roll with resistance, support self-efficacy. (Miller, W.R. and Rollnick, S., 1991)

Aversion therapy: pairing of an aversive stimulus with the behavior that is targeted for change. Can be used in combination with other forms of therapy (example – use of disulfiram)

Drug treatments for substance use. Medications: Treat withdrawal/ craving (best when used in combination with support programs)

- Anabuse (disulfiram) alcohol antagonist
- ReVia (naltrexone) block effect, alcohol craving
- Campral (acamprosate) alcohol craving
- Topomax (topirimate) alcohol
- Librium, Valium, etc. (benzodiazepines) (alcohol, etc)
- Parlodel (bromocriptine) craving (especially cocaine)
- Opiate replacement therapy: Methadone, Suboxone (buprenorphine & naloxone), LAAM (Levo-alpha acetyl methadol) (Opiate replacement therapy targets the symptoms of narcotics craving and withdrawal)
- Addiction vs physical dependence
- Concepts of "harm reduction" and "brain healing" following addiction

What can you do as a police peer support team member if (1) a person comes to you for help with an alcohol or substance use problem or (2) you know about or suspect that an officer has an alcohol or substance use problem? {discuss options – the ever present viable option is to contact your clinical supervisor and develop a plan for contact, peer support, intervention, and referral} Often, there are officers who are recovering alcoholics or alcohol-addiction sponsors within the department. They may be viable referral resources.

Alcohol and depression: link between depression and alcohol. Introduce discussion about depression and suicide.

<u>Key points</u>: substance use, alcohol use disorder, warning signs, substance effects and treatment, ADA, appropriate peer support for problematic substance use, alcohol and depression.

<u>Training objective</u>: acquaint class participants with a general view of substance use and substance use disorder; introduce several substance-related treatment modalities; discuss appropriate PST member action if substance use becomes an issue in a peer support interaction.

17. Depression and suicide

<u>Depression</u>: what is normal?

"It's perfectly natural for you to respond to the ups and downs we all experience with elation or fear. It's normal and expected for you to feel grief at the loss of a loved one, or a job, or a precious possession. It's common, and occasionally even helpful, for you to react to life's stresses, challenges, and dangers with anxiety.

- *What's NOT perfectly natural* is when those feelings persist long after the event or condition that triggered them.
- *What's NOT normal and expected* is when those feelings seem to come at you from nowhere, appearing even in the absence of obvious external triggers.
- *What's certainly NOT helpful* is feeling the weight of your emotions so heavily that they interfere with sleep, prevent you from performing daily activities, or arouse concern in the people who care about you.
- In its milder forms, depression or anxiety can make it difficult to even get yourself out of bed each morning and to go through the motions of your daily activities. Fatigue, inertia, feelings of sadness and recurring fears can hover like a rain cloud over your life.

In its more severe forms, a depression or an anxiety disorder can immobilize you, sabotage your relationships, trigger feelings of helplessness and self-destructive behavior, and perhaps even turn your thoughts to suicide". (Swartz, K. L., 2014. Retrieved 2015 from http://www.hopkinsmedicine.org)

PET image: PET scans of the brain of a depressed and not depressed person (Appendix N) - shows activity levels in various parts of the brain (Mayo Foundation, reproduced with permission) {utilize PET scan image to demonstrate brain activity difference in depressed and non-depressed persons}

SIG-E-CAPSS: mnemonic for areas of life affected by depression.

- Sleep
- Interest
- Guilt
- Energy
- Concentration
- Appetite
- Psychomotor retardation
- Suicidal ideation
- Sexual dysfunction

Depression and mania: depressive and mood disorders

Disruptive mood dysregulation disorder
Major depressive disorder
Persistent depressive disorder (formerly: dysthymia)
Major depressive episode and mania/hypomania in bipolar disorder (formerly: manic-depressive disorder)

    Bipolar I (manic episode, manic episode-major depressive episode)
    Bipolar II (hypomanic episode-major depressive episode)

Cyclothymic disorder
(specifiers)

Depression - sleep disturbances, sadness, hopelessness, loss of life's meaning, appetite disturbances, lethargy, loss of interest in previously enjoyable activities (anhedonia) including sex, poor concentration, memory, "flat affect", associated suicide risk, possible psychotic features. Specify: mild, moderate, severe, with psychotic features.

Mania - Increased energy, disorganized thinking & loose speech

- Loss of need or ability to sleep normally, logorrhea
- May be angry or euphoric & expansive
- Spends money impulsively, increased interest in sex
- Grandiose delusions, loss of judgment
- Episodic, will remit w/o treatment in most cases
- Overall, the person appears "revved up" "hyper"
- Likely a genetic and biochemical component
- Specify for mania: mild, moderate, severe, with psychotic features

Bipolar disorder - specify for bipolar and related disorders: mild, moderate, moderate-severe, severe

Suicide

In the world, a person completes suicide about every 40 seconds. In the United States, over 31,000 Americans complete suicide each year, *about 1 every 17 minutes* (estimates by the World Health Organization, http://www.who.int).

In the U.S., the Centers for Disease Control and Prevention reports:

- Overall, suicide is the eleventh leading cause of death for all Americans, and is the third leading cause of death for people 15-24 years of age.
- Although suicide is a serious problem among the young and adults, death rates continue to be highest among older adults aged 65 years and over.

- Males are four times more likely to die from suicide than are females. Females are more likely than males to attempt suicide (http://www.befrienders.org/suicide-statistics).

Best and common estimates: validity difficult to establish

1) About 80% of people who are suicidal when intoxicated are not when sober.
2) About 80% of suicidal people give some warning of their thoughts/intentions.
3) In the U.S. annually, suicides consistently outnumber homicides (about 2:1).
4) Most people who become suicidal do not remain suicidal.

Question - What are some ways in which a suicidal person may communicate their thoughts/intentions? {discuss ways}

Suicide: The *intentional* act of self-killing. Many philosophical issues and differences exist around the conception of suicide. Suicidal ideation is more prevalent in some mental disorders than others (depression and other mood disorders). Not all suicidal persons are mentally ill {provide examples}

- Suicide is frequently an act of desperation. The person often feels alone, lost, abandoned, or cannot think of viable alternatives.
- Most suicides are *not* about dying.
- Most suicides are about *stopping the pain*.

Accidental self-inflicted death (*not suicide* - intention vs. means, autoerotic behavior *fail-safe* fails, etc)

Some types of suicide:

1) blaze of glory (to be remembered, make a statement)
2) fate suicide (let another or circumstances decide)
3) suicide by cop (suicide by homicide)

4) protest suicide (political, social)
5) cause suicide (political or military objective)
6) psychotic suicide (delusion-command hallucination)
7) health issue suicide (terminal illness, health issues)
8) hopelessness suicide (mood, depression, loss)
9) revenge suicide ("get even" with or punish someone)
10) punishment suicide (punish self or others)
11) honor suicide (to avoid or in response to disgrace)
12) shame suicide (exposure of secret activity, arrest, embarrassment)
13) guilt suicide (sense of responsibility)
14) anger suicide (anger at self or others)
15) hate suicide (self-hatred)
16) life change suicide (incarceration, divorce)

There can be combined motivations for suicide. Although suicidal behavior may not appear rational to outside observers, most persons that are suicidal have a *rationale* for suicidal behavior.

Suicide prone persons:

1) particular disposition to overestimate the magnitude and insolubility of problems. Little problems seem big, big problems seems overwhelming.
2) significant lack of confidence in their own resources for solving problems.
3) tend to project a resulting picture of doom into the future.
4) the suicide-prone person has somehow incorporated the notion of the acceptability or desirability of solving problems through death.
5) death is viewed as relief.
6) psychological buffers against suicide have begun to fail. There are several predominant psychological buffers against suicide including: (1) the ability to experience pleasure - many people that are "tired of living" report that they do not attempt suicide because they continue to experience pleasure in at least some part of their lives; (2) some meaning in life – there

is something to live for; (3) concerns about family – worry about how their suicide would affect family members; and (4) religious/philosophical beliefs – suicide is prohibited by religious or philosophical beliefs.

7) hopeless and helpless perspective, loss of sense of meaning, existential meaninglessness "There's no point to life or living." (unknown author and Digliani, J.A.)

Suicidal thoughts are more common than most people believe. Such thoughts can be active or passive. They may or may not co-vary with environmental events. In those prone to suicidal thinking, suicidal thoughts often vary in intensity, frequency, and duration. Suicidal thoughts which are put into action become suicidal behavior (acting out).

Depressed and suicidal persons do not always act in ways that might be expected. If you have any concerns about a person being suicidal, ask the person about it in a caring, non-judgmental manner.

Increased levels of agitation and anxiety, and severe insomnia often precede serious suicide attempts (Fawcett, J. 2006. Retrieved 2014 from http://www.psychweekly.com)

Suicide assessment is composed of three tasks:

A sound suicide assessment is comprised of 3 components:

- Gathering information related to risk factors, protective factors, and warning signs of suicide.
- Collecting information related to the patient's suicidal ideation, planning, behaviors, desire, and intent.
- Making a clinical formulation of risk based on these sources of data. (Shea, S. C. Retrieved 2009 from http://suicideassessment.com) {Errors can occur in any of these three tasks}

<u>Suicide plan</u>:

- may be brief or elaborate.
- how does a suicide plan correlate with the likelihood of suicide? (more developed, higher likelihood of suicide)
- do suicides or suicide attempts occur in the absence of a suicide plan? (yes, impulsive)
- what can a peer support team member do to determine if a person has a suicide plan or thoughts of suicide? (ask in a caring manner)
- the contract against suicide. (effective in many cases) {discuss each item}

<u>Richard Cory</u> {read to demonstrate that outward appearance and perception of others can differ significantly from a person's internal reality}

Whenever Richard Cory went downtown,
We people on the pavement looked at him:
He was a gentleman from sole to crown,
Clean-favored, and imperially slim.
And he was always quietly arrayed,
And he was always human when he talked;
But still he fluttered pulses when he said,
"Good morning," and he glittered when he walked.
And he was rich – yes, richer than a king –
And admirably schooled in every grace:
In fine, we thought that he was everything
To make us wish that we were in his place.
So on we worked, and waited for the light,
And went without the meat, and cursed the bread;
And Richard Cory, one calm summer night,
Went home and put a bullet through his head.
(Edwin Arlington Robinson, 1869-1935. *Richard Cory*, first published in 1923)

<u>Peer support team members</u>: *Always* follow up on...

- They'll see something tomorrow...
- Things will change soon...
- Don't worry, everything will be ok...
- I can't take this much longer...
- I want you to have this...
- Will you give this to...
- I know what I have to do...
- I'm at peace with myself...

and similar statements.

<u>Emergency commitment</u>: mental health - involuntary mental health treatment and evaluation. No officer wants to go against the wishes of another officer, however in emergency situations where an officer is a danger to self and you cannot obtain voluntary compliance, you may need to use the statutory provisions for involuntary mental health treatment and evaluation. As difficult as this is, when warranted, it may save a life.

<u>Emergency commitment</u>: intoxication - involuntary alcohol and drug treatment and evaluation. {same concerns and issues as specified for mental health}

<u>QPR (Question-Persuade-Refer) strategy for intervention</u>

The four cornerstones supporting the QPR approach:

- Those who most need help in a suicidal crisis are the least likely to ask for it. Thus, we must find our at-risk citizens and go to them with help without requiring that they ask for it first.
- The person most likely to prevent you from dying by suicide is someone you already know. - Thus, those around us must know what to do if we become suicidal.
- Prior to making a suicide attempt, those in a suicidal crisis are likely to send warning signs of their distress and suicidal

intent to those around them. Thus, learning these warning signs and taking quick, bold action during these windows of opportunity can save lives.

- When we solve the problems people kill themselves to solve, the reasons for suicide disappear. Thus, crisis intervention, problem resolution and treatment save lives.
(Quinnett, P. Retrieved 2010 from http://www.qprinstitute.com/)

Helping a person that is suicidal (Appendix K) {review}

Key points: depression, bipolar disorder, suicide, suicide risk factors, suicide buffers, some types of suicide, suicide prevention, QPR, helping a person that is suicidal.

Training objective: increase comprehension of suicidal behavior; identify suicide risk factors; introduce suicide intervention strategies.

18. Police officer suicide

Police officer suicide:

- Specialized studies conducted throughout the past several years concluded that there were *141* police suicides in 2008, *143* police suicides in 2009, and *126* in 2012 (Violanti, J., et al. 2011).
- Although every suicide is a tragedy, and police officer suicide is especially painful to those in policing, these numbers are significantly lower than previous estimates. Best research: Police officer suicide rate is higher than the general population: 18 per 100,000 for police officers, 11 per 100,000 for general population (Ibid. 2011).
- Currently: no program to track the number of annual police officer suicides.

Video presentation: "Police Suicides: How many?" (National Surveillance of Police Suicides) (video available on internet)

Police suicide as a line-of-duty death? Should an officer suicide that is linked to traumatization due to an on-the-job incident or cumulative stress be considered a line-of-duty death? {classroom discussion} Currently there are no known provisions for officer suicide as a line-of-duty death.

Police officer suicide risk factors: a risk factor increases the likelihood of suicide. Risk factors are cumulative, but not necessarily causes. Many apply to all persons regardless of occupation.

- Diagnosis of depression, bipolar, anxiety, or psychotic disorder.
- Veiled or outright threats of suicide.
- Development of a suicidal plan.
- Marital, money, and/or family problems.
- Recent or pending discipline, including possible termination.
- Over-developed sense of responsibility. Responsibility absorption.
- Frustration or embarrassment by some work-related event.
- Internal or criminal investigations.
- Allegations of wrongdoing; criminal charges.
- Assaults on an officer's integrity, reputation, or professionalism.
- Recent loss, such as divorce, relationship breakup, financial, etc.
- Little or no social support system.
- Uncharacteristic dramatic mood changes. Angry much of the time.
- Increased aggression toward the public. Citizen complaints.
- Feeling "down" or "trapped" with no way out.
- Feelings of hopelessness and helplessness.
- Feeling anxious, unable to sleep or sleeping all the time.
- History of problems with work or family stress.
- Making permanent alternative arrangements for pets or livestock.
- Increased alcohol use or other substance abuse/addiction.
- Family history of suicide and/or childhood maltreatment.

- Uncharacteristic acting out; increased impulsive tendencies.
- Diagnosis of physical illness or long-term effects of physical illness.
- Recent injury which causes chronic pain; overuse of medications.
- Disability that forces retirement or leaving the job.
- Self isolation: withdrawing from family, friends, and social events.
- Giving away treasured items.
- Saying "goodbye" in unusual manner.
- Easy access to firearms (a constant for police officers).
- Sudden sense of calm while circumstances have not changed.
- Unwillingness to seek help because of perceived stigma.

<u>Officer spouse and other family members</u>: Do not hesitate to contact police support personnel if you suspect that your officer-spouse is suicidal. Call for help.

<u>Occupation may not be a significant factor in suicide</u>. Research in the area of occupation and suicide is often inconclusive and sometimes contradictory. Several past studies did not include law enforcement in the top five occupations that experience the highest rates of suicide. Instead of occupation, the following were among the top predictors for suicide:

1) diagnosable mental illness, especially mood disorder
2) co-morbid substance abuse-dependence
3) no or loss of social support
4) easy access to firearms

<u>Suicide protective factors</u>:

- effective clinical care for mental, physical, and substance abuse disorders.
- easy access to clinical intervention.
- family and community support.

- support from ongoing medical and mental care relationships.
- skills in problem solving, conflict resolution, and nonviolent handling of disputes.
- cultural and religious beliefs that discourage suicide (Catholicism – prohibition of suicide).

Video presentation – "Code 9 - officer needs assistance" (accounts of officer suicide and related commentary) (available at http//www. youtube.com)

Peer support team philosophy – suicide prevention

- the peer support team is proactive. PST members reach out to officers believed to be suicidal or otherwise experiencing difficulty.
- the PST makes an active effort to prevent police officer suicide by reducing the "seconds" of policing. (discussed in chapter 3)
- peer support team members encourage "eyes and ears" beyond the peer support team and act conscientiously upon any relevant information received from others.
- peer support team members act independently to prevent officer suicide by presenting shift briefing programs on officer suicide risk factors and suicide prevention, and making themselves available for open discussion of issues related to suicide.

Preventing police suicide – strategic summary

- Make it Safe Police Officer Initiative
- Organizational environment and COMPASS - the peer support team is an essential component of the Comprehensive Model for Police Advanced Strategic Support (COMPASS). COMPASS starts early and continues beyond retirement (Appendix L).
- Proactive Annual Check-in
- Available support services – including PST

- Knowledge of risk factors

  - In service training
  - Shift briefing training
  - Informational posters

- Peer environment – peer relationships "eyes and ears" beyond PST
- Officer and officer-family education
- Plan of action: *all officers* - reach out - know what to do

Peer support suicidal-officer action plan: What do you do if an officer to whom you are providing peer support (1) tells you that he is suicidal or (2) you suspect is suicidal?

1. Assess whether there is an imminent suicidal danger – if yes, take immediate action to assure the officer's safety – in extreme cases, this may include requesting that the officer surrender his firearm(s) for safekeeping
2. Do not leave the officer alone
3. Contact your clinical supervisor immediately - together, develop an intervention plan (may range from ongoing peer support to hospitalization)
4. Be prepared to take any action necessary to assure the officer's safety – including involuntary evaluation and treatment
5. Contact family members and other support persons as needed
6. Do not leave the officer until approved to do so by your clinical supervisor
7. Provide reassurance and caring support - provide realistic hope
8. Assist the officer to make any necessary communications with department personnel
9. Accompany the officer to any office or facility deemed appropriate for further evaluation and treatment
10. Follow up as appropriate or as directed by your clinical supervisor

The peer support team not only attempts to reduce police officer suicide by providing support services, it also becomes involved in cases of *suicide by cop* and *officer witness to suicide.*

Key points: police suicide, officer suicide risk factors, buffers against suicide, officer suicide prevention, "eyes and ears" beyond the peer support team, peer support suicidal-officer action plan.

Training objective: present information relative to police officer suicide; develop strategies for police officer suicidal behavior intervention; officer suicide prevention.

19. Suicide by cop and officer witness to suicide

Suicide by cop (SbC) involves a person who seeks death by acting in a threatening manner toward police officers with the intent of provoking officers to shoot. (http://wikipedia.org/wiki/suicide by cop)

Case of Moshe Pergament and SbC

On November 15, 1997, nineteen-year old Moshe Pergament, known as Moe to his friends, was intentionally driving recklessly on the Long Island Expressway, planning to be contacted by police. He sideswiped several cars. It was not long before his dangerous driving was reported. A short time after the reports, he was located and stopped by police. Once stopped, Moe exited his car. He pulled out a handgun. Officers ordered him to drop the weapon. He did not comply. He began to walk toward officers with his gun pointed at them. When Moe again failed to comply with the officers' orders, they fired, killing him. In Moe's vehicle, investigators found ten notes. Nine were addressed to family members and friends. One was addressed "To the officer that shot me." It read...

> "Officer, It was a plan. I'm sorry to get you involved. I just needed to die. Please send my letters and break the news slowly to my family and let them know I had to do this. And that I love them very much. I'm

sorry for getting you involved. Please remember that this was all my doing. You had no way of knowing. Moe Pergament." Pergament was holding a realistic-looking plastic replica of a silver .38 caliber revolver that he had purchased earlier the same day.

Some characteristics of persons seeking SbC:

- lower socioeconomic class male
- aggressive life-style
- violence to solve problems
- poor self-concept
- mood disorder - depression
- need to punish society or self
- need to be seen as a victim of society
- may use any means to accomplish goal including killing a hostage, police officers, etc.
  {discuss other possible characteristics –solicit class input}

SbC information

Researchers studied 707 cases of officer-involved shootings in North America from 1998 to 2006. Results showed that SbC occurs at extremely high rates, with 36% of all shootings being categorized as SbC (Mohandie K., et al. 2009). (Several older studies found incidents of SbC ranged from 10% to 26%)

Some persons seeking to be killed by the police: (1) do not possess a weapon but act as if they are armed (2) do not possess real, functional, or loaded firearms but act as if they are armed (3) are in possession of functional and loaded firearms.

Question: Why would persons in possession of a functional firearm force a law enforcement officer to kill them? Several factors:

- Social influences: Suicide remains a social taboo.
- SbC is a way of dying while *not* killing yourself.

- Fear: inability to follow through with suicide
- Religious prohibitions against suicide (SbC as a religious "loophole"?)
- Concern over insurance policy payoff
- Psychological inability to kill oneself

SbC considerations for police officers

- available lethal means for person
- officer's perception of threat
- time (can you buy time?)
- distance (can you increase distance?)
- functional verbal communication
- nonverbal behavior and posture
- cover (can you find cover?)
- back up
- officer safety
- self-defense (when other options are not available)
- officer as victim (being manipulated into shooting – having to cope with aftermath)

SbC – critical incident, peer support, possible traumatization, and interventions for officers involved in SbC

Discuss SbC as a critical incident, potential for officer-traumatization, peer support team involvement, and the application of the Trauma Intervention Program.

Officer witness to suicide

Police officers are frequently called upon to assist persons that have become suicidal. In a significant majority of these cases officers are successful in gaining the person's cooperation and the person receives appropriate professional intervention. However, not all "suicidal person" calls end this way.

Some persons will kill themselves in the presence of police officers. When officers witness a suicide, the experience can trigger a cascade of emotions. These emotions range from intense anger to feelings of guilt and sorrow. This is especially true if the officer is acquainted with the person or the officer has come to know the person during the time spent trying to keep the person from killing himself.

Some factors in the police officer emotional response to witnessing a suicide:

- Developed relationship
- Second guessing - "Did I do something that I shouldn't have, did I not do something that I should have?" This type of second guessing can lead to unjustified feelings of guilt. Remember: *You are not responsible for the person's behavior.*
- Proximity to the person
- Instrument or means of death
- Body damage, gore, blood, and death scene
- Efforts at resuscitation - failed rescue attempts
- Perceived personal danger
- Content of officer/person interaction
- Actual circumstance of the incident
- Interaction with the person's family
- Actions of other officers
- Officer's personal and family history (For example – If there has been a suicide in your family or if you lost a close friend to suicide, the incident may reactivate feelings of grief associated with your loss and the past event)

If you have witnessed a suicide:

- Accept your feelings. It is often traumatic to witness the death of another person.
- Do not blame yourself. It was the person who made the decision. We are all limited in our ability to make others act as we desire, regardless of effort.

- Do not forget that there is no perfect way to interact with a person considering suicide. All you can do is manage the interaction in the best way you can.
- Understand that you did what you thought was best to help the person.
- Take some time to process the incident before returning to shift duties.
- You will likely experience some degree of *posttraumatic stress.*
- Manage posttraumatic stress as suggested in "25 Suggestions and Considerations for Officers Involved in a Critical Incident" and "Recovering from Traumatic Stress" (Law Enforcement Critical Incident Handbook).
- Avoid alcohol or other drugs as a primary way to manage your feelings.
- Seek support: talk to a trusted peer, supervisor, friend, or appropriate family member about your experience and feelings.
- Initiate contact with your department's psychologist, peer support team, chaplain, or other available support resource.
- Become stronger and smarter

Key points: issues involved in suicide by cop, some persons seeking to be killed by police will kill others to accomplish their goal, witness to suicide, Law Enforcement Critical Incident Handbook.

Training objective: familiarize class participants with factors involved in suicide by cop and witness to suicide; present information included in the Law Enforcement Critical Incident Handbook.

20. Police primary and secondary danger, the Make it Safe Police Officer Initiative, and police culture

Discussion within this core area is based upon information included in chapter 3. {Present the notions of police primary and secondary danger, police organizational climate, and police culture. Train the elements and implementation of the Make it Safe Police Officer Initiative}

Key points: police primary and secondary danger, police culture, organizational climate, Make it Safe Police Officer Initiative, Make it Safe Police Officer Initiative implementation.

Training objective: introduce the concepts of police primary and secondary danger; comprehension of the Make it Safe Police Officer Initiative; understand the difference between police organizational climate and police culture.

21. Grief and mourning

Grief – personal, emotional responses to loss.

Mourning – public, culture-specific ways of expressing and honoring the deceased.

- There are many and varied responses to loss
- There are varying lengths of time necessary to process grief
- The "role" of guilt – implications for everyday interactions
- It may be difficult to understand the grief experience of another person

Tasks of grieving

1. Accept the reality of loss
2. Experience the pain of grief
3. Adjust to the environment in which the deceased is missing
4. Withdraw emotional investment in the deceased and recover the ability to re-invest in other relationships (Worden, J.W., 2008) {although academic in composition, the "tasks of grieving" have application in instructional settings – useful for peer support training}

Death, loss, and survivorship

1. *Learning of the death.* Shock and denial are common initial responses to death, especially if the death is sudden and unexpected. Disbelief and confusion are frequently experienced.

2. *Reactions to death.* Many factors influence how intensely we feel the loss. Among these are the nature of emotional attachment, spiritual views, the age of the deceased, how the person died, the similarity of the deceased to the living loved ones, and the extent of the void that the person's absence leaves in our life. The death of another can also trigger our own fears of death and memories of previous traumatic events or losses.

3. *Grief and mourning.* Grieving takes time. This is important to remember because American culture is not readily accepting of lengthy grieving or mourning periods. Instead, there is the idea that a person needs to put the loss behind them and get on with life. There is no single correct way to grieve. People deal with loss in different ways for different periods of time.

4. *Coping with loss.* It is common to experience powerful emotions. Confront emotions openly. Strong emotion may feel overwhelming at times, but it will naturally diminish. Let it in, let it fade (like an ocean wave). Breathe through it. Talk it out. Over time, you will be able to share pleasant memories.

5. S*pecific reactions to loss.* There are many possible reactions to loss. Common and normal reactions include sadness, crying, numbness, loss of appetite, inability to sleep, fatigue, anger, frustration, finding it difficult to be alone, or wanting to be alone. Utilizing your support system is the best way to deal with the pain of grieving.

6. *Stages of grief.* Many clinicians have identified what they refer to as stages of grief. Although such stages differ in terminology, the basic structure of the stages involve (1) an initial shock and denial, (2) a subsequent impact and suffering period, followed by (3) some adjustment and degree of recovery (similar to exposure to any traumatic event). However, grieving is a complex process; it does not progress clearly from one stage to another. It is normal to once again have feelings long thought to have disappeared.

7. *Healing.* Acknowledge and accept your feelings. You may experience seemingly contradictory feelings such as relief and sadness (for example, relief that a burden of care or the person's suffering has ended, and sadness due to the loss). This is normal. Keep in mind that your emotional attachment does not end upon the death of someone you care about. Remember, bereavement is the normal process by which human beings deal with loss.

8. *Surviving the loss.* Surviving the death of someone you care about involves honoring the memory of the person by acknowledging what the person contributed to your life (their legacy to you). From here, you can further honor the person by reengaging life. {for more information see chapter 8 of *Reflections of a Police Psychologist*}

It is important to remember that similar feelings can follow the death or loss of pets, non-pet animals, and even plants & inanimate objects that have acquired some special meaning. Brain studies show that the same neural pathways of grief are activated regardless of the loss.

Responses to death: Implications – how you choose to live your life (life by design), interactions with others, and honoring legacy of the deceased. {discuss responses to death and the implications for life}

Relate grief and loss to peer support: caring support without becoming intrusive. Sometimes just being there is enough.

Key points: grief, mourning, tasks of grieving, issues of survivorship, legacy, responses to death, implications for life, peer support during grief.

Training objective: acquaint class with cognitive and emotional aspects of death, grief, mourning, survivorship, and loss.

22. Transactional analysis for peer support

Transactional Analysis (TA) (Eric Berne, 1910-1970) is a theory which operates as each of the following:

- a theory of personality
- a model of communication
- a study of repetitive patterns of behavior

Primary concepts in TA

- Ego states, Exclusion, & Contamination
- Structure & Function
- Psychic energy & Executive
- Flow of cathexis
- Ego boundaries
- Strokes
- Transactions
- Games, Scripts, & Rackets
- Time structuring
- Contracts

The three ego states:

- Parent
- Adult
- Child

Ego states can be thought of as parts of our personality. Each ego state is made up of thoughts, feelings and behaviors that belong together.

Parent - The Parent ego state includes the thoughts, feelings and behaviors we have copied from our parents and other significant people in our lives.

The Parent Ego State is split into two categories:

- The Critical or Controlling Parent provides norms, rules, rewards, and punishment
- The Nurturing Parent loves, cares for, provides for, and protects
- The Parent is the domain of the "Taught"

Adult - The Adult is the domain of the "Reflexive" or the "Thought". Our Adult is our capacity to determine our actions on the sole basis of the received information. The Adult forms in us in the neighborhood of 10 months. It is what allows us to keep the control of the ego-state "Parent" or of the ego-state "Child".

This ego-state is often compared with a "computer" or a "regulator". It concentrates on the reality, handling as well the external information ("it is three o'clock in the afternoon", "I need more data") as the internal information resulting from the ego-states (the Child, e.g.: "I suffer, it is not fair" or the Parent, e.g.: "I am responsible").

Child - The Child ego state includes the thoughts feelings and behaviors that we developed in the past. For the most part this is developed in our childhood to enable us to thrive (cope/survive) in the world we live in.

The Child ego state is split into two categories:

- The Adapted Child composed of thoughts, feelings and behaviors learned, developed in response to other people.

- The Free or Natural Child is composed of uncontrolled, uninhibited thoughts, feelings and behaviors. A state in which people behave, feel, and think similarly to how they did in childhood.

The Child is the source of emotions, creation, recreation, spontaneity and intimacy. The Child is the domain of the "Felt". (Retrieved 2012 from http://www.transactional-analysis.info/menuglossaire.html)

The Child decides what goes into the Parent using three criteria:

1. Vulnerability of the self
2. Power of the parent figure
3. Believability of the parent figure

Concepts in ego state transactions.

Executive power and psychic energy
Ego boundaries and permeability
Exclusion
Contamination
Shifts in ego states
Lability – Sluggish cathexis

This more modern conception of TA established Controlling and Nurturing aspects of the Parent mode, each with positive and negative aspects, and the Adapted and Free aspects of the Child mode, again each with positive an negative aspects.

Transactions under analysis

Strokes are the recognition, attention, or responsiveness that one person gives another. Strokes can be positive (nicknamed "warm fuzzies") or negative ("cold pricklies") and conditional or unconditional. A key idea in TA is that people hunger for recognition, and that lacking positive strokes, they will seek whatever kind they can, even if it is a negative kind recognition.

Transactions may be complementary, crossed, or ulterior

A complementary transaction is characterized by a response being sent from the ego state which received the stimulus, and sent to the ego state from which the stimulus originated.

A crossed transaction results when the response is directed at an ego state other than the one from which the stimulus was generated

Ulterior transactions contain a social message as well as a psychological message: For example: A: "I need you to stay late at the office with me." (Adult words), body language indicates sexual intent (flirtatious Child). B: "Of course." (Adult response to Adult statement), winking or grinning (Child accepts the hidden motive).

Three rules of transactions in TA communication:

1. So long as the transactions remain *complementary*, communication may continue indefinitely.
2. Whenever the transaction is *crossed*, a breakdown (sometimes only a brief, temporary one) in communication results and something different is likely to follow.
3. The outcome of transactions will be determined on the *psychological* level rather than on the *social* level.

What events and people trigger your Parent and Child state?

- Do you assign responsibility equally?
- Do you have to be in control?
- Do you feel forced into taking control?
- Do you have a hard time making decisions and try to get others to make them for you?
- Do you feel fundamentally you're not as good as others?
- What might these issues bring out in other people, in reaction to you?
  (From: Theramin Trees, TA training)

Games In TA

"A game is an ongoing series of complementary ulterior transactions progressing to a well-defined, predictable outcome. Descriptively, it is a recurring set of transactions...with a concealed motivation... or gimmick."

"Because there is so little opportunity for intimacy in daily life, and because some forms of intimacy (especially if intense) are psychologically impossible for most people, the bulk of the time in serious social life is taken up with playing games. Hence games are both necessary and desirable ..." (Berne, E. 1964).

- Purpose of games: *To promote the life script.*
- Will go on as long as someone is willing to be victimized.
- The drama triangle: On each end are roles that we play in life. One is the persecutor, another is the victim and the last is the rescuer.
- If anyone in this triangle changes roles, the other two roles change as well. (Retrieved 2012 from http://karpmandramatriangle.com/)

PERSECUTOR - "It's All Your Fault" VICTIM - "Poor Me" RESCUER - "Let Me Help You" (Steiner, C., 1990) (James, M. & Jongeward, D., 1978)

Steiner on the drama triangle... "the Victim is not really as helpless as he feels, the Rescuer is not really helping, and the Persecutor does not really have a valid complaint."

- Withdrawal
- Ritual
- Activity
- Pastimes
- Games (and scripts)
- Intimacy

Transactional Analysis Life Positions

> I'm ok, you're ok
> I'm ok, you're not ok
> I'm not ok, you're ok
> I'm not ok, you're not ok (Harris, T.A., 1969)

How might you apply TA in peer support? {solicit class input}

Application of TA in peer support

- If you apply TA in your life, it will help you to help others
- Helps to keep you focused in desired ego state
- Conceptual model: provides a "way to think" in your life and a way to support others…but it is not the only way
- Not offensive – does not pathologize
- Normally does not invoke defensiveness
- Provides a framework for discussion of patterns of behavior
- Assists with plans of action and desired change
- Lends itself well to "Immediacy"
  {to the class} Can you think of other applications for TA in peer support?

TA class activity

- Groups of three: PST member, person seeking peer support, observer. Exchange roles upon instruction.
- Begin Child-Child complementary transaction.
- Move to Adult-Adult complementary transaction.
- Observer: notice transactions and determine if a transaction was crossed. Prepare to report and discuss observations to class group.

Key points: principles of transactional analysis, ego states, ego state transactions, rules of TA communication, drama triangle. Limit to second-order analysis.

Training objective: explain transactional analysis in terms that make it possible for class participants to utilize the concepts in peer support.

23. Critical incident debriefing

The process of debriefing should be utilized only under selected critical incident circumstances. There are several other support interventions which may be used in cases where debriefing is deemed less than ideal.

Peer support team debriefings and clinical debriefings: Peer support teams may or may not become involved in the facilitation of critical incident debriefings. Possible: (1) peer support team debriefing – facilitated by peer support team members. Implemented when officers are not directly involved in the incident (for example, officers exposed to a particularly gruesome suicide) (2) clinical debriefing – facilitated by a licensed clinician. Implemented when officers are directly involved in the incident (for example, an officer defends himself with lethal force). These examples represent a general guideline. In many cases, clinical judgment must be exercised to determine if debriefing is appropriate and if so, what type of debriefing should be utilized. Peer support team members participate in and contribute to debriefings facilitated by licensed clinicians.

Incidents being considered for debriefing should be evaluated by an experienced licensed clinician to determine if a debriefing is warranted. If yes, the clinician approves the debriefing and determines what type of debriefing should be utilized.

Models for debriefing

1. Phase Model
2. Freezeframe Model

Phase model (the incident is processed in some variation of the following phases)

- Introductory Phase
- Fact Phase
- Feeling Phase
- Response Phase
- Information Phase
- Reorganization Phase (Critical Incident Stress Debriefing – CISD) (Mitchell, J.T. 1983: Mitchell J.T. and Everly, G.S., 1996)

Freezeframe model (the incident is processed through time frames)

The incident is -
1) organized into "frames"
2) processed within frames
3) all elements are processed
4) process until frame is "completed"
5) the group guides the frame process
6) the facilitator "freezes" frames as appropriate
7) education, strength, and resiliency are part of frame processing
8) need for follow up is assessed (Digliani, J.A., 1992)

Recent concerns of debriefings – (1) disrupting the normal psychological trauma integration process of participants, (2) the retraumatization of individual debriefing participants, and (3) the vicarious traumatization of a previously non-traumatized involved participant or support person.

The current research involving the efficacy of critical incident debriefings remains confusing. There are several studies which seem to support the effectiveness of debriefing and several which suggest that debriefing as currently practiced does little to help and may in fact be harmful to at least some participants. This last finding is especially troublesome because of the ruling ethic in medicine and psychology which is "First, do no harm."

In reference to critical incident debriefing, the following can be stated with some degree of confidence:

- Debriefing seems to help many debriefing participants "feel better."
- Anecdotal information demonstrates that most debriefing participants find the debriefing helpful.
- "Feeling better" and being "helpful" does not establish the clinical efficacy of critical incident debriefing.
- Critical incident debriefing may help some participants and not others.
- Critical incident debriefing may not be benign. It may create difficulties for some participants.
- CISD phase debriefing is only one element of the broader conceptualized Critical Incident Stress Management model (CISM). When CISD is applied independently of CISM, the efficacy of CISD may be altered. This may account for some of the research findings involving CISD.
- There is no conclusive evidence that debriefing of any kind prevents the development of posttraumatic stress disorder or other stress-related disorders.
- To minimize potential harm, all debriefing participants should be assessed for participation appropriateness prior to the debriefing.
- Participation in debriefing should be voluntary.
- *Resiliency debriefings* (which avoid phases & frames and instead focus on health & recovery) seem to avoid the possible pitfalls of traditional debriefings.
- Only additional well-designed research will clarify the efficacy and dangers of critical incident debriefing as currently practiced by most agencies.
- Police agencies should consider the above information prior to establishing critical incident debriefing policies. The appropriateness of *peer support team debriefings* should be assessed and approved by a mental health professional. Appropriately trained peer support team members should debrief with caution and only with clinical oversight.

Resilience

"Resilience is the process of adapting well in the face of adversity, trauma, tragedy, threats or significant sources of stress — such as family and relationship problems, serious health problems or workplace and financial stressors. It means "bouncing back" from difficult experiences. Research has shown that resilience is ordinary, not extraordinary. People commonly demonstrate resilience. Many studies show that the primary factor in resilience is having caring and supportive relationships within and outside the family. Relationships that create love and trust, provide role models and offer encouragement and reassurance help bolster a person's resilience" (Retrieved 2011 from http//www.apa.org).

Keys to successful debriefings: relax, stay attentive, and trust the group process.

Key points: peer support team debriefing, clinical debriefing, phase and freezeframe debriefing, concerns about debriefing, resiliency debriefing.

Training objective: introduce types of debriefing, debriefing concerns, and debriefing dynamics.

24. Keeping yourself healthy

Peer support: keeping yourself healthy and self-care. Self-care - appropriate assertiveness, proper personal boundaries, balancing life stressors, etc. (self-care is not selfishness – being selfish is getting what you want regardless of effect on others).

Review elements of self-care:

- Exercise regularly. Maintain an active lifestyle.
- Eat and drink a healthy diet.
- Maintain interests, hobbies, and relationships outside of policing.

- Do not hesitate to ask for support during stressful times.
- Practice what you have learned in PST training. No one is immune to stress.
- Utilize healthy stress management strategies that have worked for you.
- Experiment with new stressor management strategies.
- Maintain or reclaim your life, family, relationships, and career.
- Utilize and implement *Some Things to Remember.*
- Keep a positive attitude.
- Do not expect perfection – from yourself or others.
- Develop a sense of humor. Learn to laugh at yourself.
- Remain mindful of your personal boundaries.
- Apply and practice *life-by-design.*
- Support one another - seek support from other peer support team members.
- Remain mindful of the *Imperatives (Communication, Occupational,* and *Relationship)*

Key points: difference between self-care and selfishness, factors for self-care.

Training objective: enhance personal philosophy of self-care within and without the role of peer support.

End of PPSTT: Summary, Comments, and Questions

{Trainer provides a brief summary of the most important peer support principles, a review of the interpersonal dynamics of peer support, and allows time for end-of-program comments and questions.}

"Completion of Police Peer Support Team Training" certificates are awarded.

CHAPTER 3

The Make it Safe Police Officer Initiative

The *Make it Safe Police Officer Initiative* grew out of the conceptions of police primary and secondary danger. The distinction between police primary and secondary danger was inspired by the Below 100 initiative program. Therefore, to fully understand primary-secondary danger and the Make it Safe Police Officer Initiative, it is imperative to examine the Below 100 Program. The best way to accomplish this is by looking at the history of Below 100 in its own words.

The History of the Below 100 Program

"Like many good ideas, the Below 100 initiative came out of a conversation around a dinner table. In April 2010, several contributors to Law Officer Magazine and friends were enjoying a dinner together at the International Law Enforcement Educators and Trainers Association (ILEETA) Conference. There had been a spate of officer deaths, and clearly, everyone at the table was concerned. Major Travis Yates of the Tulsa Police Department made a statement that caused everyone to pause...

'If we would just slow down, wear our seatbelts and clear intersections, we could get our line of duty deaths to Below 100 a year'

The idea of Below 100 began at that table and continues today and it's evolved into Below 100 Program, an initiative that aims to reduce the line of duty deaths to below 100, a number not seen since 1944. If you're reading this, consider yourself part of this conversation.

We can do this. We've done it before. In 1974, the all-time high year for officer deaths, 278 were killed in the line of duty. Innovations in training, emergency medicine and vehicles, as well as the development of ballistic armor, all contributed to bring this number down. We've averaged about 150 officers killed per year in the last ten years. Together, we can bring that number to below 100.

We have identified five key tenets by which we can improve officer safety—areas where we can make a difference. Below 100 isn't about statistics. It's about each and every officer, trainer and supervisor taking individual and collective responsibility for the decisions and actions that contribute to safety.

For those in a leadership position, Below 100 means supporting a culture of safety throughout your department. Make doing the right thing so ingrained in your personnel that it becomes the norm and not the exception. Just as importantly, hold accountable those who stray outside what should be common sense. Often, a private word with a misguided officer is all it takes to correct his or her misperception. Below 100 is committed to providing you the tools and resources you need to make a culture of safety thrive throughout your department.

Finally, Below 100 is a challenge that recognizes each officer death as a tragedy. It's our duty to face down death and protect the innocent when called to do so. It's a fact: Good cops will die each year. But working together—and only by working together—we can keep our streets and ourselves safer."

The Five Tenets of Below 100

1. Wear Your Belt

It might sound simple to you, even unnecessary, but the truth is too many agencies don't mandate belt wear. And even among those that do, many officers ignore policy because the culture doesn't value it. *The truth:* Seatbelts save lives.

2. Wear Your Vest

We know vests save lives. We know that bullets can fly when we least expect it. Add to that the fact that body armor can improve your likelihood of surviving a car accident or other traumatic event and you quickly see why you must wear it. Always. Period.

3. Watch Your Speed

Why do cops drive fast? Because they can, right? Well, driving faster than what conditions warrant is a sure way to get in trouble. Of course there are times when getting on scene quickly is critical. But these times are rare. Too often, officers are speeding—just because they can. In the process, they are putting themselves and the public at perilous risk *for no good reason.*

4. WIN—What's Important Now?

It's a simple question that can elicit profound results. It's a question that will lead to deliberate action, not reaction. If you are constantly prioritizing what's most important, you won't have time for the distractions that can get you in trouble, hurt or killed.

5. *Remember:* Complacency Kills!

Chief Jeff Chudwin perhaps said it best: "Complacency is among the most dangerous and insidious threats we face because it lays us open to all others." Complacency is why police officers think they can go without vests and seatbelts. It's why they think they can speed and allow themselves to be distracted. To quote Chief Chudwin again: "Complacency will kill you." (retrieved from www.below100. com) (reprinted with permission)

> Below 100 is an initiative to reduce police line-of-duty deaths to fewer than one hundred per year.

Recognizing Below 100

I became aware of the Below 100 initiative shortly after it was published. As a police psychologist and former police officer, each of the five tenets made sense. They are easily understood and readily implemented. Most of all, I liked that Below 100 identified some things that officers could do for themselves to increase their margin of safety. In short, Below 100 identified risks inherent in policing (like responding to emergencies) and offered ways to mitigate them (wear your seat belt, wear your vest, watch your speed, what's important now, avoid complacency).

Police primary danger

I soon realized that Below 100 addressed several elements of the *primary danger* of policing. The primary danger of policing is comprised of the inherent risks of the job, such as working in motor vehicle traffic, working in bad weather, confronting armed and violent persons, being a target of disgruntled persons, and so on. You need only to read a newspaper or watch a news broadcast to understand the primary danger of policing. Unfortunately, due to the differences among people and the divergence of various philosophical and belief systems, the risks that comprise the primary danger of policing will never be zero. Police officers counterbalance the risk inherent in policing by applying the three T's of policing— Training, Tactics, and Technology. The three T's represent factors designed to reduce the probability that officers will be injured or killed in the line of duty. They are most effective when they achieve a standard of quality, and when police officers properly use and engage them. For example, officers do not benefit from ballistic vests if they do wear them (Technology and Below 100 Tenet 2) and officers do not benefit from trained and proven officer-safety strategies if they do not engage them (Tactics and Below 100 Tenet 5).

The primary danger of policing is comprised of: (1) physical primary danger and (2) psychological primary danger. The physical primary danger of policing is characterized by the examples previously mentioned. They represent circumstances in which an officer can be physically harmed. Most officers are at least somewhat trained to manage most of the circumstances that comprise the physical primary danger of policing. Such training usually includes instruction in safety driving, traffic control, use of safety equipment, disaster and hazardous material spill response, infectious diseases, officer safety and self-defense, arrest and control, and firearms. Because the type, quality, and subject matter of such training can vary widely among agencies, some officers are better prepared than others to deal with the physical primary danger of policing. The Below 100 program helps officers to deal with training disparities by identifying five basic tenets that can be readily utilized by all officers regardless of their previous training; it reminds officers to apply fundamental safety strategies and interpersonal officer-safety principles. It is in this way that Below 100 addresses the physical primary danger of policing.

The psychological primary danger of policing is related to, but distinguishable from the physical primary danger of policing. The psychological primary danger of policing is represented in the increased probability that due to the nature of policing, officers will be exposed to critical incidents, work-related cumulative stress, and human tragedy. This higher probability of exposure results in an increased likelihood that officers will suffer psychological traumatization and stressor-related disorders. It is the increased likelihood of psychological traumatization and the increased likelihood of experiencing stressor-related disorders that comprises the psychological primary danger of policing. Another way of saying this is that the physical primary danger of policing constitutes a work environment that generates the psychological primary danger of policing.

Police psychological primary danger

The existence of an increased probability that police officers will suffer work-related psychological traumatization and stressor-related disorders (psychological primary danger) has been known for some time (Reiser, M. 1973). Many modern law enforcement agencies have recognized this feature of policing and have attempted to address it. They have addressed it by initiating stress management training, contracting for employee assistance counseling programs, creating peer support teams, developing officer-involved critical incident protocols, and providing access to police psychologists. Some departments have gone so far as to engage comprehensive mental-wellness programs. These programs start at employment and extend beyond retirement (COMPASS is one such program). Regardless of the specific type or combination of police stress management programs, all have as their goal the prevention or reduction of the possible undesirable effects of the psychological primary danger of policing.

Similar to police physical primary danger and the Below 100 initiative, properly developed support programs designed to help officers cope with the psychological primary danger of policing are effective only to the degree that they are personally implemented or utilized. Many officers benefit from these programs on a regular basis, some do not. Some officers choose not to engage the support programs available to them, even when confronting very difficult circumstances. Why? The answer to this question is associated with an insidious *secondary danger* of policing that has its foundation in the primary danger of policing (Figure 1).

Police secondary danger

In the years before Below 100, as a police psychologist, I had become painfully aware of a danger to police officers beyond that inherent in policing...themselves. The significance of this danger is readily observed in the number of recorded annual police officer suicides. For the years in which there is reasonably reliable officer-suicide/officer-line-of-duty-death data (2008, 2009, & 2012), the number of police officer suicides exceeded the number of officers killed by felonious assault or by accident. In fact, for these years, the number of police suicides exceeded the number of officer deaths from felonious assault and accidents *combined**. With practical extrapolation, for most years of at least the past two decades, it is reasonable to conclude that suicide has been the number one killer of police officers. (*Based upon statistics reported by Officer Down Memorial Page, excluding officers that died as a result of 9/11/2001 related illness and heart attack, and the National Surveillance of Police Suicide Study) (http://www.odmp.org) (http://www.policesuicidestudy.com).

I have treated police officers that had become suicidal. I have also witnessed the aftermath of completed officer suicides. Some of these officers spiraled inexorably downward while attempting to put up a good front. They tried to look good and expended much effort to hide the fact that all was not well. They needed help but would not ask for it. If their spouse, coworker, or friend offered help, they rejected it. If anyone tried to compel them to seek help, they reacted forcefully against them. They concealed enough of their state of mind that involuntary treatment was not an option.

Why was it so difficult for these officers to ask for help? Why was it so difficult for these officers to accept help when offered, even if they felt incapable of asking for it? Why did some of these officers act upon suicidal thoughts instead of reaching out for support? These are important and probing questions. A large part of the answer to these questions is traumatization, anxiety, depression, and other mood disorders - and everything that these conditions entail. But there is another contributing and influencing factor – and it is already known to every police officer.

As I thought about Below 100 and its common sense approach to reduce police officer line-of-duty deaths, I realized that a common sense approach was also needed to help prevent police officer suicide. If Below 100 had the potential to reduce officer line-of-duty deaths by addressing features of police physical primary danger, then another initiative could be developed to address the secondary danger of policing.

What is this secondary danger? The secondary danger of policing is a powerful conceptual undercurrent that pervades the policing profession. It is often unspecified and seldom discussed. It is an artifact of the police culture and is frequently reinforced by police officers themselves. The secondary danger of policing is the idea that equates *"asking for psychological help"* with *"personal and professional weakness."* Secondary danger is reinforced by the fear of department or peer ridicule or reprisal for seeking psychological help. This is the contributing and influencing factor mentioned previously, and it is the factor that every police officer knows only too well.

Interestingly, fears of department or peer ridicule or reprisal are seldom observed in officers confronting what they view as physical illness or physical injury. This is because physical illness and physical injury retain a personal and social acceptability not yet observed in perceived psychological conditions. Unfortunately, there still exists a bias in the personal and social acceptability of what is viewed as "psychological" versus "physical" when it comes to police officer illness and injury.

How serious is police secondary danger? So serious that some officers will act out their suicidal plan or suicidal impulse instead of asking for help.

The policing profession is not alone. There is a similar secondary danger in numerous other occupations, and it is also a characteristic of some dysfunctional family and other social systems.

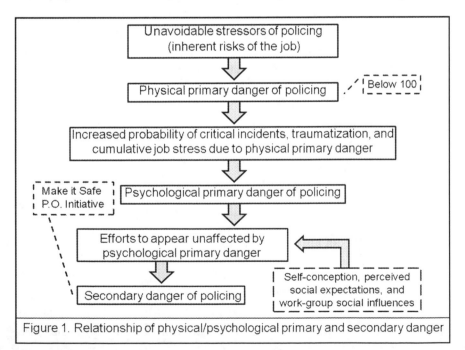

Figure 1. Relationship of physical/psychological primary and secondary danger

Comprehensive action

To act comprehensively, law enforcement agencies must not only concern themselves with training officers how to do the job - thereby addressing the physical primary danger of policing. They must also initiate and maintain programs aimed at officer mental wellness - thereby addressing psychological primary danger and the secondary danger of policing. Such wellness programs should include efforts to:

(1) educate officers in stress management, stress inoculation, posttraumatic stress, posttraumatic stress disorder, traumatization, alcohol and substance abuse, the warning signs of depression, and officer suicide prevention
(2) engage more pre-emptive, early-warning, and periodic officer support interventions
(3) initiate incident-specific protocols to support officers and their families when officers are involved in critical incidents
(4) create properly trained and clinically supervised peer support teams
(5) provide easy and confidential access to psychological support services
(6) enhance the agency organizational climate so that officers are encouraged to ask for help when experiencing psychological or emotional difficulties instead of keeping and acting out a deadly secret.

The three "seconds" of policing

Secondary danger - the idea that equates "asking for psychological help" with "personal and professional weakness."

Secondary injury - the harm that can be caused to officers when they are poorly treated following involvement in a critical or otherwise stressful incident.

Secondary trauma - also known as vicarious trauma - the indirect traumatization that can occur when a person is exposed to others who have been directly traumatized. Secondary trauma is a real concern for the spouses and family members of officers that have been involved in a critical incident, peer support team members, as well as previously non-traumatized officers and others participating in departmental critical incident debriefings.

The Make it Safe Police Officer Initiative

The Make it Safe Police Officer Initiative (MISPOI) represents a concerted effort to reduce the secondary danger of policing. It was developed in 2013 and consists of 12 elements. It is designed to promote police officer mental wellness and reduce the frequency of police officer suicide. The core of the initiative is simple - *make it safe for officers to seek or ask for psychological support.*

The Make it Safe Police Officer Initiative seeks to:

(1)   make it personally and professionally acceptable for officers to engage peer and professional psychological support services without fear of agency or peer ridicule or reprisal.

(2)   reduce officer fears about asking for psychological support when confronting potentially overwhelming job or other life difficulties.

(3) change organizational climates that discourage officers from seeking psychological help by reducing explicit and implicit organizational messages that imply asking for help is indicative of personal and professional weakness.

(4) alter the profession-wide law enforcement culture that generally views asking for psychological help as a personal or professional weakness.

(5) improve the career-long psychological wellness of officers by encouraging police agencies to adopt long-term and comprehensive officer-support strategies such as the Comprehensive Model for Police Advanced Strategic Support.

The twelve elements of the Make it Safe Police Officer Initiative

The Make it Safe Police Officer Initiative encourages:

(1) every officer to "self-monitor" and to take personal responsibility for his or her mental wellness.

(2) every officer to seek psychological support when confronting potentially overwhelming difficulties (officers do not have to "go it alone").

(3) every officer to diminish the sometimes deadly effects of secondary danger by reaching out to other officers known to be facing difficult circumstances.

(4) veteran and ranking officers to use their status to help reduce secondary danger (veteran and ranking officers can reduce secondary danger by openly discussing it, appropriately sharing selected personal experiences, avoiding the use of pejorative terms to describe officers seeking or engaging psychological support, and talking about the acceptability of seeking psychological support when confronting stressful circumstances).

(5)   law enforcement administrators to better educate themselves about the nature of secondary danger and to take the lead in secondary danger reduction.

(6)   law enforcement administrators to issue a departmental memo encouraging officers to engage psychological support services when confronting potentially overwhelming stress (the memo should include information about confidentiality and available support resources).

(7)   basic training in stress management, stress inoculation, critical incidents, posttraumatic stress, police family dynamics, substance use and addiction, and the warning signs of depression and suicide.

(8)   the development of programs that engage pre-emptive, early-warning, and periodic department-wide officer support interventions (for example, proactive annual check in, "early warning" policies designed to support officers displaying signs of stress, and regularly scheduled stress inoculation and critical incident stressor management training).

(9)   agencies to initiate incident-specific protocols to support officers and their families when officers are involved in critical incidents.

(10)   agencies to create appropriately structured, properly trained, and clinically supervised peer support teams.

(11)   agencies to provide easy and confidential access to counseling and specialized police psychological support services.

(12)   officers at all levels of the organization to enhance the agency climate so that others are encouraged to ask for help when experiencing psychological or emotional difficulties instead of keeping and acting out a deadly secret.

> Asking for help does not mean "unfit for duty"

Implementing the Make it Safe Police Officer Initiative

Implementing the Make it Safe Police Officer Initiative is not difficult. The elements of the Initiative are easily implemented by initiating processes, strategies, and programs already well known to law enforcement agencies.

The Initiative is not an "all or nothing" proposition. Various elements of the Initiative can be implemented independently of one another. Although it is best to move forward with the entire Initiative, a partial implementation is better than no implementation.

There is no "one right way" to implement the Initiative. It is ok to be creative. Make the *Make it Safe Police Officer Initiative* work for you.

<u>Considerations and recommendations for implementing the elements of the Make it Safe Police Officer Initiative</u>

(1) The Initiative encourages: every officer to "self-monitor" and to take personal responsibility for his or her mental wellness.

<u>Implementation</u>: Many officers are pretty good at picking up signs of distress in others. But as an officer, have you ever thought of applying this skill to yourself? Accomplishing this simply requires you to make an honest and ongoing self-assessment. Although denial can be or become an issue, many officers know when they are experiencing stress or trauma-related difficulty. However, knowing you are having difficulty is not enough. You must also know what to do about it and be willing to take action. One of the things that you can do about it is to talk to someone. Allow yourself to seek appropriate support and assistance.

(2) The Initiative encourages: every officer to seek psychological support when confronting potentially overwhelming difficulties (officers do not have to "go it alone").

<u>Implementation</u>: Why limit yourself to personal stress management ideas and strategies? You can supplement your solo stress

management efforts by engaging outside support. Outside support comes in many varieties, ranging from talking with a trusted friend to professional counseling. Many times just talking it out will help you to see things differently and help you to feel better, The next time you feel stressed, take a chance. Talk to someone you trust. You may be pleasantly surprised at the outcome.

(3) The Initiative encourages: every officer to diminish the sometimes deadly effects of secondary danger by reaching out to other officers known to be facing difficult circumstances.

Implementation: Even if an officer is not exhibiting outward signs of distress, if you know that he or she is dealing with circumstances that would be difficult for nearly everyone, try reaching out. Too often, officers will shy away from other officers in distress for a variety of reasons, including not knowing what to say or do. But think about this – during years of policing and psychological practice I have had officers time after time talk about how an unanticipated kind word from another officer made a positive difference. It does not take much, and it's not like you need to form a life-long relationship. Sometimes just a few supportive words can make a remarkable difference.

(4) The Initiative encourages: veteran and ranking officers to use their status to help reduce secondary danger (veteran and ranking officers can reduce secondary danger by openly discussing it, appropriately sharing selected personal experiences, avoiding the use of pejorative terms to describe officers seeking or engaging psychological support, and talking about the acceptability of seeking psychological support when confronting stressful circumstances).

Implementation: Veteran and ranking officers are in a unique position to influence the police culture generally and organizational climate specifically. They can do this for better or for worse. If you are a veteran or ranking officer, make a positive difference. As mentioned, you can help to reduce secondary danger by openly discussing it, appropriately sharing selected personal experiences, avoiding the use of pejorative terms to describe officers seeking or engaging psychological support, and talking about the acceptability of seeking psychological support when confronting stressful circumstances.

(5) The Initiative encourages: law enforcement administrators to better educate themselves about the nature of secondary danger and to take the lead in secondary danger reduction.

Implementation: The conceptual distinction between police primary and secondary danger is relatively new. Police administrators should think through the notions of police primary and secondary danger, take the lead, and consider ways to reduce secondary danger within their agencies.

(6) The Initiative encourages: law enforcement administrators to issue a departmental memo encouraging officers to engage psychological support services when confronting potentially overwhelming stress - the memo should include information about confidentiality and available support resources.

Implementation: This is easily accomplished by administrators. All it takes is an understanding of what support services are available, learning about the limits of confidentiality, and a commitment to write and distribute such information in a departmental memo. If you are a police administrator, whether or not you support the entire Initiative, implementing this element would clarify your position, help to define your philosophy, contribute to a supportive organizational climate, and help to reduce secondary danger. A memo from the chief that identifies support services and encourages their use expresses a caring attitude and lets officers know that it is ok to seek support. This element alone has significant potential to help officers in distress. (see Police Administrators and the Make it Safe Police Officer Initiative).

(7) The Initiative encourages: basic training in stress management, stress inoculation, critical incidents, posttraumatic stress, police

family dynamics, substance use and addiction, and the warning signs of depression and suicide.

Implementation: In nearly every jurisdiction there are qualified persons that are willing to train officers in the specified areas. Resources for this training include local or regional mental health facilities, community psychologists and counselors, area community colleges, local universities, academy cadre, and specially trained officers already within the department. Training in these areas should begin in recruit academy and continue throughout an officer's career.

(8) The Initiative encourages: the development of programs that engage pre-emptive, early-warning, and periodic department-wide officer support interventions (for example, proactive annual check in, "early warning" policies designed to support officers displaying signs of stress, and regularly scheduled stress inoculation and critical incident stressor management training).

Implementation: Initiating pre-emptive, early-warning, and periodic support programs is nothing new for law enforcement agencies. Many departments offer stress management refresher training periodically and have early warning officer-assist policies and programs already in place. These programs are designed to help officers cope with everyday stress and the potentially overwhelming stress of policing before it becomes an issue.

(9) The Initiative encourages: agencies to initiate incident-specific protocols to support officers and their families when officers are involved in critical incidents.

Implementation: It takes some work but it is possible for an agency to develop a standardized protocol for dealing with critical incidents. The protocol can define "critical incident" and "officer-involved" to best fit departmental standards. It can also specify when the protocol should be engaged. Critical incident protocols not only help to standardize incident investigation, but can also be designed to reduce second injury, secondary trauma, and secondary danger. Incident protocols can be developed by and applicable to individual law enforcement agencies or they can be developed by and applicable to multiple jurisdictions. To implement this element of the Initiative, it takes someone to introduce the concept, secure administrative support, develop the protocol and have it approved, then put it into effect. Agencies with an officer-involved incident protocol have used a committee of officers and other professionals to develop it. Such committees have included officers, investigators, supervisors, administrators, district attorneys, peer support team members, and police psychologists.

(10) The Initiative encourages: agencies to create appropriately structured, properly trained, and clinically supervised peer support teams.

Implementation: The efficacy of police peer support teams is well understood by police psychologists and many police administrators. To be most effective, police peer support teams must be formally established in policy and function under departmental written guidelines. Peer support team members should be trained by qualified personnel and receive ongoing training and clinical supervision. Clinical supervision provides a "ladder of escalation" and "support for the supporters." Several states have enacted legislation which provides members of police (and other) peer support teams with a degree of statutory confidentiality.

(11) The Initiative encourages: agencies to provide easy and confidential access to counseling and specialized police psychological support services.

Implementation: Most departments provide insurance coverage for private psychologists and counselors, and many have developed Employee Assistance Programs. Some agencies also provide in-house psychological services. Regardless of the services provided, they must be easily accessible and remain confidential within the limits prescribed by law if officers are to view them as viable resources.

(12) The Initiative encourages: officers at all levels of the organization to enhance the agency climate so that others are encouraged to ask for help when experiencing psychological or emotional difficulties instead of keeping and acting out a deadly secret.

Implementation: Police officers must remain aware that even seemingly innocuous verbal exchanges and unintentional nonverbal gestures can contribute to police secondary danger. To avoid this, officers of all ranks must act conscientiously, proactively, and consistently to reduce police secondary danger. This requires increased personal awareness and may require a significant shift in thinking for some officers. In this way, officers can positively affect their agency's organizational climate and thereby, the police culture.

> The effects of the Make it Safe Police Officer Initiative are cumulative: the more elements implemented, the greater the effect.

Police culture

There is a great deal of officer-support variability in law enforcement agencies. Just where a department falls on the "officer-support" spectrum seems to depend upon the department-endorsed perspective of various elements of the police culture. If this sounds confusing, it is because the term "police culture" is abstract and not easily defined. Some definitions are general: "Police culture is a type of organizational culture that contains unwritten roles and social codes that dictate the way that a person within the culture will function, as well as building a strong sense of solidarity among the group and a will to conform" (retrieved from http://www.ask. com/government-politics/police-culture). Other definitions appear to capture only the more controversial and less flattering aspects of policing: "The term police culture can refer to several different aspects of policing. It can refer to the "us versus them" attitude that is attributed to police forces almost everywhere, whereby "them" can be variously meant "society at large," "criminals" and "senior police officials". Police culture can also refer to police attitudes towards the use of their discretionary powers, especially where the end (protecting society from criminals) is thought to justify the means (for example, unlawful searches, excessive use of force and untruthful testimony). Finally, police culture can refer to the strong feeling of loyalty towards and social solidarity with fellow officers, a feeling which goes beyond what is normally encountered among employees, even other professionals" (retrieved from http://sociologyindex.com/police_culture.htm). I have yet to find a sociological definition of police culture that includes "service" and "protecting others at the risk of one's life."

There are definitions of police culture that include the phrase "code of silence." In these definitions, "code of silence" is interpreted as the unwritten rule of one cop not "snitching" or "squealing" on another. It wouldn't take long to find historical examples of this type of code of silence in policing (as well as in many other professions). However, most modern police agencies have zero tolerance for officers covering up or remaining silent for one another. Officers that continue this practice in cases where they are expected or required to take action do so at their own risk. Many officers have been disciplined, including having their employment terminated or being criminally charged, for covering up, remaining silent, or otherwise not meeting their professional obligations.

No matter how the perceived police code of silence is defined, there is another feature of the code that is less obvious. This feature is insidious and often influences officers in ways they themselves do not understand. It is the psychological extension of the code that transforms "don't tell on others" to "don't tell on yourself." It is in this way that the historical police code of silence has encouraged police officers to suffer job and life related stress, trauma, and depression in silence...even when their very lives are at risk. It is in this way that the outdated and unprofessional police code of silence, once a significant component of the police culture, has contributed and continues to contribute to police secondary danger.

When considering the perceived code of silence and other negative aspects included within the various definitions of police culture, there have been and likely will always be some police officers who betray the true values of policing. These bad cops abuse their authority, tarnish the badge, and damage the reputation of all police officers. Some are unethical, some are unprofessional, and some engage in criminal activity. The policing profession is on constant alert to indentify such officers and to remove them from the ranks of the nation's finest.

Police organizational climate

Regardless of how police culture is defined, individual *organizational climate* can be different. Organizational climate is reflected in the stated and unstated acceptances and practices that are characteristic of any particular agency. These acceptances and practices may or may not correspond with the broader conception of police culture. How does organizational climate relate to police culture? - change enough police organizational climates in any particular direction and you will change the police culture in a similar manner.

When it comes to addressing police secondary danger, organizational climate is the key. Some departments seem entirely unaware of secondary danger and therefore have done little to confront it. Other departments have intentionally or unintentionally created climates that reinforce and strengthen secondary danger (a very undesirable circumstance). Still others have recognized the stressor features of policing and have implemented programs that are intended to support comprehensive officer wellness. These departments have developed an "it's ok to take care of yourself" organizational climate. Some have gone farther and have established a "we expect you to take care of yourself and we support your efforts to do so, physically and psychologically" organizational climate. These departments have taken a significant step forward in the reduction of secondary danger. However, no matter how well-designed these programs might be, their effectiveness will be undermined to the extent that intra-agency mistrust exists. For example, the best intentioned departmental programs implemented by the most enlightened administrators will be limited in what they can accomplish if officers dismiss them or refuse to utilize them due to fear of administrative or peer reprisal or ridicule. Eliminating these fears, encouraging mutual trust within the department, positively changing organizational climate (and thereby the police culture), and reducing secondary danger are goals worthy of every modern-day law enforcement agency.

Officers and the Make it Safe Police Officer Initiative

For some officers, it is not a concern about administrative or peer reprisal or ridicule that keeps them from reaching out when they are in stressor-related trouble. It is the way in which they think about themselves as persons and police officers that restricts their behavior. Too many officers maintain the mindset, "I'm a cop, I give help, I don't ask for help" or "I will handle this on my own even if it kills me." This way of thinking is not only characteristic of some officers, it is also reinforced by other similar-thinking or bravado-persona officers. For these officers, this combination of personal belief and peer reinforcement makes the probability that they will seek appropriate support in times of difficulty nearly non-existent. To do better, officers must reconsider and re-conceptualize what it means to be a police officer. Everyone has a limit to what they can successfully cope with alone. A healthier police mindset includes a willingness to seek appropriate psychological support when things get tough.

It helps to remember that all occupations have a core of unavoidable stressors. When dealing with the unavoidable stressors of policing, some officers believe "If you can't stand the heat, get out of the kitchen." This is a colorful way of expressing the belief that if "you can't handle the stressors of policing, get out" (other police expressions used to capture this idea are "suck it up" "man up" "cowboy up" and "put on your big girl panties" or leave). But think about this for a minute. Does it make sense? Does it make sense to deny that *any* person can be overwhelmed by a constellation of job and life stressors? Does it make sense to believe that if you or another officer feel overwhelmed, your only option is to get out? And just what does "get out" mean...quitting, retiring, suicide? Thinking that you must "handle it or get out" creates a false dilemma and is psychologically naïve. The "handle it or get out" way of thinking contributes to and strengthens police secondary danger.

While getting out of a stressful environment is a recognized stressor management strategy (the strategy of *withdrawal*), it is not the only one. When thinking about the "kitchen" and "heat", withdrawal may be a viable option but other strategies should also be considered. How about, "let's lower the heat in the kitchen when possible, and when not possible, let's help ourselves to better manage the heat." The Make it Safe Police Officer Initiative is designed to help officers lower and better manage the heat.

If you are an officer fortunate enough to work for an agency that has implemented viable officer-support programs, remember Make it Safe Police Officer Initiative element 1. Police department good intentions and supportive programs can only do so much. Officers themselves must assume responsibility for their health and mental-wellness; police departments must assume responsibility for making it safe for officers to do so. To help accomplish this, officers are encouraged to bring the Make it Safe Police Officer Initiative to the attention of their administrators. Administrators are encouraged to take the time to consider it.

The ultimate goal of the Make it Safe Police Officer Initiative is to positively alter the police culture by creating a new profession-wide standard for officers in distress. This new standard would make it agency-safe and personally-acceptable for officers to seek or ask for psychological help when experiencing difficulty. In spite of the fact that changing the police culture is a daunting task, we can begin this effort by first shifting organizational climates. Every officer in every department, in every assignment and at every rank, has the potential to influence organizational climate. Together we can make a difference. Together we can positively change the police culture.

Reprinted with permission
from the State of New Jersey
Police Suicide Task Force

Police Administrators and the Make it Safe Police officer initiative

Police administrators are in a unique position to reduce the secondary danger of policing within their agencies. As mentioned in element 6 of the Make It Safe Police Officer Initiative, something as simple as a memo to employees can go a long way to encourage officer wellness and diminish secondary danger. Such a memo can be sent out initially, periodically, and in response to a critical incident. For example:

> "I just wanted to reach out and acknowledge everyone who played a part in the response to the fatal train/ pedestrian accident in (name of town) last night - whether you were on scene, on the phone or just

working in support of the incident. Those types of incidents can take an excessive toll on responders... In the wake of incidents like these, remember to take care of yourselves and don't be afraid to reach out to the members of the peer support team if you just want to talk about your experience with someone." (from a memo sent February 10, 2015 by Sheriff Justin Smith, Larimer County, Fort Collins, CO) (implements elements 4, 6, 10, and 12 of the Make it Safe Police Officer Initiative) (reprinted with permission)

CHAPTER 4

More Reflections of a Police Psychologist

The following are a collection of thoughts related to various observations. They are not presented in any particular order. Similar to many ideas expressed in this book, most have relevance to those working outside of policing.

Criticism and police action

There are persons that will criticize nearly every police action. Consider the following: an officer is dispatched to investigate a man standing on a corner of a busy intersection. The man was reported to have been jumping into the street, swinging a hammer, and yelling obscenities at drivers of passing cars. Dispatch advises the assigned officer that a backup unit is currently unavailable but will be dispatched as soon as possible. The assigned officer, fearing for the safety of the man and passing motorists, knowing that a backup unit will be sent, acknowledges the call and proceeds to the intersection. As the officer approaches the intersection, he observes a man doing just what was reported – jumping into traffic, swinging a hammer, and yelling obscenities at passing drivers. The officer parks a short distance from the man and exits his police vehicle. The man, upon seeing the officer, advances toward him while swinging the hammer and yells "I'll kill you!" The officer commands the man to stop. He doesn't. The man continues to advance. The officer draws his weapon, points it at the man, and again commands him to stop. He doesn't. The man, still advancing, again yells "I'll kill you!" The officer fires and the man is killed.

Everyone would agree that a hammer can be a deadly weapon. The officer had a right to defend himself with lethal force. However, in this case there would almost certainly be a group of people that would voice the opinion "Why did the officer have to shoot him? He only had a hammer. The cop should have taken the hammer away from him. I've seen that guy. Everyone knows that he would never really hurt anybody. What kind of training do these cops get? These cops are trigger happy and out of control."

Now consider the same scenario except that the officer does not shoot. The man advances and is chemically sprayed. No effect. The officer deploys his electronic control device. No effect. The man attacks the officer. They fight hand-to-hand. The man repeatedly strikes the officer with the hammer. The officer is killed. Other officers arrive. The man drops the hammer and is arrested.

In the second scenario there would almost certainly be a group of people that would voice the opinion "Why didn't the officer shoot? Didn't he know that a hammer is a deadly weapon? I've seen that guy. He's strange. What kind of training do these cops get? These cops are not well trained. He should have shot the guy."

Interestingly, the theoretical group of people that might criticize the officer in each of the presented scenarios are likely to include many of the same persons!

Although these scenarios are hypothetical, they represent a category of circumstances that are familiar to most police officers. Officers are well aware of the social reality that there are persons that will criticize their actions regardless of the outcome...even in cases where officers are killed while trying not to kill someone.

Judged by the outcome: the *officer's dilemma*

Related to the "criticism and police action" social reality is the "judged by the outcome" social phenomenon. "Judged by the outcome" is associated with the fact that every officer, everyday, necessarily makes decisions based upon information that is often incomplete and sometimes inaccurate. If the outcomes of the decisions made under these circumstances are viewed as "good" or desirable, the consequences are normally viewed as acceptable or justified. There is no or little criticism or social sanction. However, if the outcome is viewed as "bad" or undesirable, officers are subject to consequences ranging from public derision to internal or criminal investigation. This is in spite of the fact that similar decisions made under similar circumstances can produce outcomes that are viewed as good in one situation and bad in another. How can similar decisions made under similar circumstances produce different outcomes? Differential outcomes are possible due to the factors that are unknown to the officer at the time decisions had to be made.

The "judged by the outcome" social phenomenon is representative of the *officer's dilemma*. The officer's dilemma is the social reality that officer-actions will be judged by some persons and at least in part, upon its outcome... *an outcome that is impossible for the officer to know beforehand.* So what is an officer to do?...this is the dilemma. To address the dilemma, most officers rely on policy and procedure, and their training and experience. Most officers realize that there are no outcome guarantees, just probabilities.

In its worst formulation, the officer's dilemma causes a cognitive distraction which can lead officers to make poor decisions, including hesitating when the situation might best be addressed by a rapid response. In its mildest form, officers are overly concerned with how every decision and subsequent action might be evaluated by others.

Regarding the officer's dilemma, there are two things officers need to keep in mind: 1) police officers cannot safely make decisions solely based upon what they believe others might think or how their actions might be later evaluated, and 2) police officers will continue to be held accountable for their actions. Therefore, officers must be prepared to make decisions based on the best information available at the time decisions need to be made. They must also remain current on procedural law and departmental policy and procedure. This is because, ultimately, regardless of the circumstances or outcome, officers must be prepared to explain or discuss why they did or did not do something in any presenting circumstances.

The decisions of police officers can have serious and sometimes dire consequences, especially when they involve the use of lethal force. However, police officer's decisions should be judged upon the circumstances as they were understood by the officer at the time the decision had to be made, and not upon the outcome.

Being judged by the outcome is not limited to policing. There are numerous other professions within which judgment-by-outcome is a noteworthy social factor.

Passive-aggression and appropriate assertiveness

When persons becomes upset, angry, or otherwise disenchanted with another person viewed as their superior, some choose to engage in *passive aggressive* behavior. A "superior" is any person that is viewed as having a status greater than oneself in at least one specific area. A superior may be a parent, sibling, spouse, supervisor, friend, a person of higher organizational rank, and so forth.

Passive aggressive behavior is seen most often in situations where active (direct) aggression is likely to have undesired consequences. Passive aggressive behavior is a complex social interaction pattern. So complex in fact, that the very term "passive aggressive" seems contradictory.

Passive aggressive interactions are best described as the *indirect* expression of anger, resentment, or negative feelings. Indirect expression of these emotions can take many forms including procrastination (sometimes referred to as "dragging your feet"), intentionally not performing or performing poorly, feigned helplessness, intentional "forgetfulness", talking badly behind someone's back, and employing the "silent treatment." Persons that are most likely to engage passive aggressive behavior share several personality characteristics. These include being sullen, argumentative, resentful, and stubborn. They also tend to avoid responsibility, do not easily accept corrective feedback, and generally do not relate well to authority figures. They often feel underappreciated, which is a feeling often used to rationalize passive aggressive behavior.

Most persons that are prone to engage passive aggressive behaviors are not always passive aggressive. They might be passive aggressive in one situation may become actively aggressive in another. Much depends on the perceived status of the other person and the perceived possible consequences. Therefore, a person that deliberately fails to perform part of a work assignment because he is angry at his supervisor (and later claims to have simply "forgotten"), might yell at his wife for not having dinner ready on time. Of course, he might also continue his passive aggressive behavior at home. He might not yell at his wife. Instead, he might express his displeasure over the late dinner by brooding, scowling, refusing to eat when dinner is ready, and refusing to talk with her.

Repetitive patterns of significantly dysfunctional passive aggressive behavior have been clinically recognized as a personality disorder for many years. The original Diagnostic and Statistical Manual of Mental Disorders (DSM), published in 1952, listed "passive-aggressive personality" among the conditions of "Personality trait disturbance" (36-37). In its most recent clinical formulation (1987) the diagnosis of Passive Aggressive Personality Disorder (PAPD) was defined as behaviors that "are inflexible and maladaptive and cause either significant functional impairment or subjective distress" (335) and that represent a "pervasive pattern of passive resistance to demands for adequate social and occupational performance, beginning by early adulthood and present in a variety of contexts" (357) (DSM-III-R). This changed in 1994, when the diagnosis of PAPD was moved to the appendix of the fourth edition of the DSM as a "diagnosis requiring further study" due to the lack of diagnostic clarity (DSM-IV). This effectively removed PAPD from the list of distinct personality disorders. To date, PAPD has not been reinstated as an independent personality disorder; however, clinicians can still diagnose passive aggressive behaviors that meet the criteria of a personality disorder under the "other specified and unspecified personality disorder" provisions of the current DSM (DSM-5).

Passive aggressive behavior is often observed in organizations that maintain a clearly defined rank structure (like the military and police agencies). This is because levels of rank are clearly established and the chain of command is normally unambiguous.

In such organizations, passive aggressive behaviors are more likely because there are significant consequences and inherent career risks in being actively aggressive with persons of higher rank.

Everyone has some capacity for passive aggressive behavior - even officers known for their good work and motivation. For example, consider the following actual occurrence: a nighttime squad of officers captured and arrested a group of burglars that had been breaking into businesses for several previous weeks. They caught them in the act. The police response and subsequent arrests were generated by a call from a citizen who had observed in-progress suspicious circumstances. The officers felt very good about these arrests. They had broken up a small-time burglary ring. The next night at shift briefing, the officers were still talking about the arrests made the night before. They were ready to start their shift and felt highly motivated. The shift sergeant overheard the squad talking enthusiastically about the arrests. During the shift briefing, in reference to the arrests, the sergeant addressed the squad and said "Don't get too excited, you didn't do much. You guys were just lucky." The briefing room fell silent. You could literally see the change in the squad's demeanor in response to the sergeant's remarks. A short time later, the sergeant dismissed the squad to begin the night's patrol. While the squad was walking to their police vehicles, one of the most productive and normally motivated officers of the squad who was involved in the arrest of the burglars the night before, said "I'm not doing anything tonight. Why should I work hard to make him (the sergeant) look good." The other officers of the squad agreed. The officers were true to their word - not much self-initiated activity was generated that evening. Incidentally, although the sergeant was working the night of the burglary arrests, he was not involved in the response or apprehension.

Sergeants (and any first-line supervisor) are in a singular position to affect the morale and motivation of their subordinates. Their behaviors and supervisory style can create or suppress a productive and job-satisfying work group micro-environment. They can do this regardless of the department's overall state of morale (macro-environment), although a generally poor level of departmental morale makes any sergeant's effort to create and maintain a positive micro-environment more difficult.

In the incident mentioned, the sergeant's unfortunate remarks that the officers "didn't do much" and were "just lucky" were responsible for *motivation deflation*. They increased the probability that the officers would feel unappreciated and undervalued by their supervisor - and it resulted in the officers' loss of motivation and passive aggressive behavior. The sergeant failed to *communicate to motivate.* What could the sergeant have done to avoid motivation deflation? What could he have said to communicate to motivate? All he needed to do was to say something as simple as "Guys, good work last night. Let's keep it going" and his squad would have worked the shift with eagerness and enthusiasm.

> A good sergeant can buffer officers from a poor chief, but a good chief cannot buffer officers from a poor sergeant

Better than active or passive aggression is *appropriate assertiveness.* When persons are appropriately assertive they first decide if assertion is necessary. After all, not every issue warrants confrontation. Some things can be "let go" without resulting in resentment, active or passive aggressive behavior, or long lasting difficulties. If it is decided that an issue merits assertion, appropriately assertive persons select a suitable time and place to initiate discussion with the involved person.

In appropriate assertiveness, there is no intention to harm, embarrass, or "get even" with the person. The primary goals of appropriate assertiveness are conflict resolution and relationship improvement.

To be appropriately assertive (as opposed to inappropriately assertive):

1. avoid initiating discussion when angry.
2. remain calm and respectful during the discussion.

3. present the facts as you know them; state "facts" tentatively, allowing for the possibility that some of your information may be inaccurate.
4. be honest about your personal view and emotional experiences.
5. remain open minded.
6. listen to (not just hear) the perspectives of others.
7. avoid blaming, shaming, and scolding.
8. strive to strengthen or repair the relationship.
9. move on from perceived transgressions.
10. work for a positive outcome.

In general, appropriately assertive persons make a genuine effort to resolve any difficulty meriting confrontation by properly standing up for themselves while respecting the rights and opinions of others.

Keep in mind that being appropriately assertive:

1. is a skill to be learned, and once learned, it can be continually improved.
2. may not be well received by those confronted.
3. may have unanticipated consequences.
4. does not mean you will get what you want (like agreement, acknowledgement of improper behavior, change in future behavior, an apology, etc).
5. is a life-by-design endorsed personal value.

So, in the case of the officers and their sergeant, as an officer, do you think that you have appropriately confronted the sergeant? If yes, where, when, and how? If not, do you think you could have "let it go" without experiencing motivation deflation? Would you have resorted to passive aggressive behavior?

In the end, relying upon active or passive aggression to deal with the inevitable stressors and conflicts of life are more likely to create problems than to diminish them. Learning to be appropriately assertive decreases the probability of active or passive aggression, and increases the probability of successful conflict resolution.

Other people are not you

Other people are not you. Who would argue with the validity of this statement? On the surface it appears so obvious that further discussion appears unnecessary. But *knowing* that other people are not you is insufficient to make much difference in your life. To really benefit from this potentially profound insight, you must come to *understand* that other people are not you. This understanding will help you to maintain better personal boundaries, avoid frustration, become more tolerate of others behavior, and better manage your life.

Other people are not you - this means that at times, others will wait when you would act. They will act when you would wait. They might remain in circumstances that you would abandon, and abandon circumstances in which you would remain. This is because, due to many factors, there is a wide range of variability among individuals.

The variability among individuals is seen most clearly in the area of interpersonal relationships. When it comes to interpersonal relationships, it is sometimes easy to "know" what others should do. For the most part, we think that others should do what we think we would do in similar circumstances. It is much more difficult to try to understand why they are doing what they are doing. This is especially true when we are having difficulty seeing things from their perspective.

How is it possible for you to "know" what others should do in circumstances that cause them great ambivalence? Why do they not see their situation in the way you see it? Why do they not act as you would (or believe you would) act? The answers to these questions are psychologically and sociologically complex. For current purposes, suffice it to say that there are two primary factors that make it possible for you to "know" what other persons should do in circumstances that create indecision for them: (1) you do not have the emotional investment or attachments that exist for them and (2) you will not experience the real-life consequences that they will experience upon making a decision. Therefore, the personal process of making any significant life decision is fundamentally different for the involved person than it is for any outside observer.

Most persons will eventually decide things for themselves. Even when they plead "Tell me what to do" and you unwisely tell them, they seldom act in accordance with any or all aspects of your advice. This is because it is likely that they have already considered what you are advising and your advice will not eradicate their ambivalence. In any event, your advice will likely be rejected. The reasons for rejection usually include the less desirable consequences of the action you are advising - which are also the cause of the person's underlying ambivalence! Therefore, the verbal exchange, "tell me what to do" followed by "you should do X" (and the person does not do X) can become a repetitive game that soon becomes frustrating for both the seeker and provider of advice. Alternatively, if you advise the person to do X and the person does X, and things do not go well, the failure will likely be assigned to you..."I listened to you and now look where I'm at." Unless your advice consists of factual information that advises a person on how to proceed with something already decided, telling others what to do seldom results in any long-term positive outcomes. Deciding things for people that are capable of deciding themselves is inherently dysfunctional, encourages dependency, and suppresses the development of self-responsibility and personal independence. This is not a desirable outcome. This is why the "tell me what to do" - "you should do X" pattern of interpersonal interaction is rarely seen in healthy functional relationships.

Sometimes people get stuck. They seem unable to make a decision. They remain indecisive regarding undesirable life circumstances for lengthy periods of time. Meanwhile, days, months, years, even decades can pass. Some persons argue that remaining indecisive is a type of decision - a decision to endure the circumstances. In these cases, it is only when (and if) the *undesirable* becomes the *intolerable* that persons will implement change. Making decisions and engaging behavior that alters circumstances that have become intolerable often fosters change in the lives of involved others (like when a person decides to leave an abusive spouse).

In the end, it is wise to remember that others may not think what you think, may not feel what you feel, may not value what you value, and may not act how you might act. This is because they live in a different psychological and sociological world. This is because they are not you.

Couples, patterns, and teamwork

Ever wonder why things seem to go so well at the beginning of a relationship only to deteriorate as time passes? This early period, when it seems that things could not be much better, can last from weeks to years. It is sometimes called the "honeymoon" period, and it is characterized by the best behavior of each person and a high degree of tolerance for the idiosyncrasies of each other. Then, in many relationships, something seems to change. There are greater demands for perfection, less flexibility, and less tolerance for other-person differences. This results in more disagreement and discord. In some cases, the discord is sufficiently intense to cause relationship disintegration.

Couples relationships are characterized by recurring patterns of behavior. Because they are recurring, these behavioral patterns frequently lead to predictable outcomes. Pattern outcomes range from *functional* to *dysfunctional*. It is the dysfunctional patterns within a relationship that undermine the honeymoon period.

If you are trying to improve your relationship by altering a dysfunctional pattern, it is often helpful to share information with your partner. The *Marriage and Couples Exercise* is designed to help you share and focus important relationship information.

The Marriage and Couples Exercise is a useful tool for relationship enrichment. It sometimes helps to start with something more easily addressed and move on to the more significant issues. Although the Exercise is designed for use outside of professional counseling, you should seek professional support if you feel that your relationship issues are beyond what you can positively address on your own.

The Marriage and Couples Exercise works best when both persons remain kind and caring, open minded, and non-defensive during discussion. To help you do this, remember the Relationship Imperative: *Make it Safe*. Make it safe for your partner to honestly communicate with you. Making it safe is an essential component of all functional relationships.

For relationship enhancement it is often helpful to think, "It's me and you against the dysfunctional pattern" instead of "It's me against you, and you against me." The first way of thinking makes you and your partner allies for desired change, instead of adversaries that see things differently. When you ally with your partner, some very positive things can happen. Why? Think about what members of a team do when a team member is experiencing difficulty. They come to his or her aid. It is the same for marriage and other romantic relationships. In functional relationships, spouses come to the aid of their teammate.

Marriage and Couples Exercise

Instructions for partners: In section 1, write in what your partner might do differently to help you. Try to be specific, for example "vacuum the carpet at least once a week" or "not raise your voice when we talk." Once section 1 is completed, exchange information verbally or by reading each other's responses. Based upon what your partner has written in section 1, write what you are willing to do differently for your partner in section 2. For example "I will vacuum the carpet at least every Tuesday." Once section 2 is completed, discuss your responses with one another. Negotiate if necessary. Work until you have a positive plan for pattern change. Once the Exercise is completed, stay true to your word – follow through on what you have agreed to do differently.

Section 1: It would help me if you would:

(1) _____

_____

(2) _____

_____

(3) _____

_____

<u>Section 2: To help us enhance our relationship, I am willing to</u>:

(1) _____
_____

(2) _____
_____

(3) _____
_____

Couples and money

Money is one of the most common areas of conflict for couples. When it comes to money, there is the potential for conflict over who earns money, the amount of money being earned, how money is being earned, how money should be spent, and how money should be saved. Some couples have one income source. Other couples have multiple income sources. Some couples choose to share or combine their money, while others keep their money separate. Finding a money arrangement that works for both persons in a marriage is a primary challenge for all couples. Once couples find the money strategy that works best for them, conflict over money normally diminishes.

Most couples have rules pertaining to money. An example of a couple's rule pertaining to money is "all major expenditures require mutual agreement." The couple must then decide what constitutes a major expenditure.

Most adults enjoy having some unencumbered or "free" money. Free money is money that a person is free to spend, save, or do otherwise, *without spousal approval or criticism.* For couples, the actual amount of free money is usually dependent upon income and personal monetary strategies, but the *amount* of free money is less significant than the *idea* of free money – and the idea of free money works best when each person in the couple has some.

The free money idea works well for couples because most persons value different things (remember, other people are not you). Therefore, if combined money is spent on something that one person values and the other does not, it often results in the other person viewing it as an unnecessary expenditure, or worse, a waste of money. If one person in the relationship consistently out-spends the other on things he or she values (including donation to charities, gifts for others, etc) using combined money, it can cause a one-sided general dissatisfaction within the relationship. Couples that employ the free money concept can avoid this potential conflict.

If you do not have free money in your relationship, talk to your spouse about it. If both of you are open to the idea and it is possible within your monetary circumstances, select an amount and make it free money. Try the free money strategy on a three-month trial basis. You are likely to be satisfied with the result. If you are not satisfied with the free money idea, you can always return to what you were doing.

When it comes to money, to help maintain a baseline of enhanced self-esteem, productive self-care, and personal independence in healthy functional relationships, each person of every couple should have an amount of free money.

Tunnel thinking – tunnel feeling

Tunnel thinking and tunnel feeling are the cognitive and emotional equivalent (respectively) of tunnel vision. Most everyone is familiar with the concept of tunnel vision. It is best described as the phenomenon wherein most of what is in a person's visual field goes unnoticed due to an enhanced focus on a particular object or area within the visual field. Tunnel vision is well known to police officers. It is one of the most frequently officer-reported visual distortions experienced during a critical incident.

Tunnel thinking is like tunnel vision except that it involves an enhanced focus on a single or small number of related thoughts. Tunnel thinking is most often observed in persons under duress. It is a significant component of moderate to severe depression and frequently involves thoughts of worthlessness and death. Tunnel feeling is similar to tunnel thinking in that the person has difficulty feeling anything other than a single or small number of related emotions. Tunnel thinking and tunnel feeling are often linked to one another. For instance, a person that has tunnel thoughts of worthlessness and death often feels worthless and feels a degree of desire to die.

Tunnel thinking is distinguishable from obsessional thinking. In obsessional thinking, a person is obsessed with a single thought or a small number of thoughts but is normally capable of accessing and considering other thoughts. In tunnel thinking, the ability to access and consider other thoughts is more limited. The same is true of tunnel feeling. The range of emotion in tunnel feeling tends to be more restricted than it is in other range-of-emotion constrictions.

In the tunnel thinking and tunnel feeling associated with depression, depressed persons sometimes pursue their death directly. In these cases, the person is *actively suicidal*. Actively suicidal persons represent a significant danger to themselves. The danger they represent to themselves is positively correlated with the degree of active suicidality - the more actively suicidal, the more self danger.

Some actively suicidal persons select a means for their death that is likely or certain to kill others, like a pilot intentionally crashing a passenger airplane. When actively suicidal persons choose a means of death that will likely or certainly kill others, they may (1) have psychologically accepted the death of others as an undesirable but unavoidable component of their suicidal plan, (2) have rationalized the consequences, for example, a pilot that intentionally crashes a passenger airplane who believes that "everyone on this plane has problems. If I crash it and they die, they'll be better off," (3) want to make a statement through the death of others, (4) want to take others into a perceived afterlife, (5) want to experience a final sense of control and control over others, (6) simply not care about whether others live or die, and so forth. There are many other possible variables that factor into actively suicidal scenarios wherein others may die. These variables include preferred means of death and perceived available means of death. Statistically, most actively suicidal persons do not select a means of death that would likely harm others.

Some depressed persons desire to die but are not actively suicidal. Persons that have a desire to die but are not actively suicidal are *passively suicidal*. Passive suicidality may be conscious or unconscious. When persons are passively suicidal, they do not plan to kill themselves. Instead, they wish their death through other means. For example, one passively suicidal person reported praying that the airplane in which she was a passenger would crash. This is an example of *conscious passive suicidality*. She wanted to die, she was aware of her desire to die, and she wished for death through a means other than killing herself. Interestingly, in this case, there were no thoughts or concerns for the lives of the other passengers. This was not because she was an uncaring person or that she wished others would die. It was because in this state of mind she could not think or feel past her anguish and despair. She had become so focused on her desire to die that consequences other than that desired (her death) simply did not enter her awareness. So it is for all persons in this state of mind - such is the power of tunnel thinking and tunnel feeling.

Some passively suicidal persons, like some persons that are actively suicidal, can be aware of the additional consequences related to their wish to die. If these consequences are not enough to alter their current experience or expression of tunnel thinking and tunnel feeling, they have somehow come to terms with the means of their wish to die.

APPENDIX A

Peer Support Team Brochure

City Police Department Peer Support Team for You And Your Family

WELCOME

The City Police Department Peer Support Team (PST) welcomes you to the Police Department. Whether you are a new employee or a seasoned veteran, the PST stands ready to assist you in times of stress, crisis, or problems in everyday living. You can also contact us if you just want to talk.

Members of the PST are specifically trained in peer support and are available to all employees of the Police Department and members of their families.

Should you or your family need any type of personal support, please contact us directly. You may talk with any PST member, and you do not need prior approval from Supervisors or Trainers. We are available all hours, day or night.

Peer Support

Traditionally, emergency services personnel have turned to each other for support. Peer support is based upon the idea that talking to a trusted peer can be helpful when confronting challenging personal or social circumstances.

PST Confidentiality

Issues discussed during peer support interactions are considered confidential within the limits prescribed by law and department policy. Safeguarding information acquired in such settings is deemed a primary obligation of PST members.

Peer Support Team members reveal information involving others only with the consent of the person, except in those unusual circumstances where: (1) a person is mentally ill and presents an imminent danger of suicide or homicide, or a person is gravely disabled, (2) a person is intoxicated and there is an immediate danger to self or others, (3) there is actual or suspected child abuse or neglect, (4) there is actual or suspected elder abuse or exploitation, (5) there is information indicative of any criminal conduct (C.R.S. 13-90-107(m)).

Members of the Peer Support Team who are peace officers are also required to take action, including arrest, in domestic violence cases where there is probable cause that a crime has been committed.

Peer Support Team members also have an obligation to discuss information involving peer support interactions with police psychologist, Dr. X. This is because Dr. X serves as the Clinical Supervisor of the Peer Support Team.

TEAM MEMBERS

(Insert names of PST members) (optional)

Getting Help

No one can live through a stressful situation for you; however you do not have to go through it alone. Allow your family, friends and peers to help. As a member of the Police Department, the following support resources are available to you:

Peer Support Team

To contact members of the Peer Support Team you may contact them directly. You may also page through Dispatch (if applicable) (include other contact options).

Name of agency psychologist (if applicable)

(Insert psychologist contact information)

Employee Assistance Program (if applicable)

(Insert EAP contact information)

Agency Chaplains (if applicable)

(Insert Chaplain contact information)

Community Resources Included in the Police Department Insurance Plan

Consult insurance-plan information for benefits

(Include other available support resources)

Appendix B

Psychologist and Recruit/Training Officer Liaison (PATROL)

The PATROL program is proactive and brings the police psychologist and new officers together early in the training process. The first contact occurs within the recruit pre-service skills academy. This presentation is comprised of a group orientation, followed by training in various stress-related topics. Following pre-service academy orientation and training, the police psychologist meets individually with new officers at least once during each of the first three field training officer (FTO) phases. Spouses are invited to attend any or all of the FTO phase meetings.

The PATROL program is easily adapted to the Patrol Training Officer (PTO) training phases. In the PTO program the meetings between the psychologist and new officers would be scheduled for the Orientation Phase and all or some combination of Phases A, B, C, and D.

The PATROL program is founded upon four principles: (1) that counseling can be supportive and proactive, (2) that the training experience of new officers is enhanced by meetings with the police psychologist, (3) that problematic behavior can be targeted for change from a multidimensional perspective, and (4) that early exposure of new officers to the police psychologist increases the probability that officers will seek counseling when it is likely to help.

Below is a descriptive outline of the PATROL program.

Orientation and Training. During orientation and training many issues are discussed. Topics include career choice, adult learning, stress and anxiety management, family dynamics and issues, being new to the community, departmental policy, FTO program, critical and traumatic incidents, trauma intervention program, PATROL, and services of the peer support team and police psychologist.

Meeting during FTO Phase I. Information discussed during phase meetings is confidential. Reconciling the reality of police work with expectation is the primary focus of the Phase I session. Within this framework, officer observations are processed, officer safety is discussed, stressor and anxiety management strategies are assessed, application of skills is encouraged, and features of reputation and work ethic are explored. Family issues are assessed. Specific problematic issues are identified and addressed.

Meeting during FTO Phase II. Issues surrounding the Phase II session frequently involve motivation and persistence. Some new officers report that field training is more rigorous or stressful than anticipated. Officers with prior experience sometimes struggle with being in training again. The psychologist works to enhance motivation by pointing out successes, commenting on the growing sense of competence, discussing alternative learning and stressor management strategies, identifying problem areas, and designing specific interventions. Emphasis is placed upon the assumption of responsibility, officer discretion, and the appropriate application of authority.

Meeting during FTO Phase III. The Phase III session centers on rehearsal for Phase IV. In addition to stressor management and job skill enhancement, officers are encouraged to scan their knowledge and skill level for areas in which they need improvement. They remediate these areas or bring them to the attention of their FTO for assistance. The FTO then works to provide the new officer with the appropriate review, practice, exposure, or experience necessary to succeed in Phase IV. In preparation for Phase IV, new officers implement the three Rs: *Review, Rehearse, Repeat.*

Phase IV. Checkout. Upon successful completion of Phase III, the new officer is advanced to Phase IV. As the focus of this phase is independent behavior, Phase IV meetings are optional. Phase IV appointments may be requested by the new officer, by the new officer's FTO, or recommended by the police psychologist. Upon successful completion of Phase IV, the officer assumes duties as assigned.

PATROL Program Features

The PATROL program is flexible and may be adjusted to meet individual needs. For instance:

1. More than one meeting with the psychologist per phase may be requested by the new officer or FTO.
2. Family members of new officers may initiate independent counseling programs.
3. The FTO may attend any or all (or portions) of the sessions if requested by the new officer.
4. The psychologist may share information with FTOs and supervisors upon request of the new officer (with waiver of confidentiality) when warranted.

5. The FTO and new officer may arrange joint sessions with the police psychologist to address a specific performance issue.
6. The new officer may initiate a comprehensive counseling program. Such programs can involve other significant persons and extend beyond FTO training.
7. If the new officer is failing to progress as expected, counseling can be integrated into a remedial plan. Such plans may involve family members of new officers.
8. If the new officer fails to succeed in the FTO program, counseling may assist the officer and/or FTOs in processing the officer's resignation or termination.

APPENDIX C

Model Peer Support Team
Operational Guidelines

(Colorado – for other states, edit as necessary)

The Peer Support Team functions as a peer support and debriefing resource for personnel of the police department and their families. In order to effectively meet this responsibility, the Peer Support Team (PST) adopts the following operational guidelines.

I. Peer Support

Members of the Peer Support Team are committed to functioning within the limits of their peer support training. Peer support interactions may continue as an adjunct to comprehensive professional counseling or any other ongoing professional or self-help program.

II. Clinical Supervision

The Peer Support Team is clinically supervised by the department-appointed licensed mental health professional. This person is designated the PST *Clinical Supervisor.* The clinical supervisor is responsible for the clinical supervision and the ongoing in-service training of the Peer Support Team.

III. Team Coordinator

The PST team coordinator is appointed by the chief of police. The team coordinator is the primary spokesperson for the PST and represents the team in matters involving department staff, agency, and interagency issues. The PST team coordinator is administratively responsible for the PST's operational status. The team coordinator and the clinical supervisor function as co-chairpersons during PST team meetings.

Assistant team coordinators will be selected in compliance with department policy. Assistant team coordinators assist the team coordinator and clinical supervisor in the performance of their duties. They function as the PST coordinator in the absence of the team coordinator. An acting team coordinator will be appointed by the team coordinator during periods of absence of the team coordinator and assistant team coordinators.

IV. Primary Obligations of Peer Support Team Members

Professional Supervision

Peer Support Team members have a primary obligation to communicate their peer support activities to the PST clinical supervisor. Due to the varying nature of the issues involved in peer support, some peer support team member activity may be communicated at regularly scheduled PST meetings. In circumstances where more timely supervision or consultation is needed, team member activity should be communicated to the clinical supervisor as soon as practical. In emergencies or circumstances involving critical intervention, PST members should contact the clinical supervisor immediately.

If the information pertaining to a member's peer support activity is assessed by the team member as inappropriate for discussion in a regularly scheduled group PST meeting, the PST member should arrange to discuss the interaction(s) with the clinical supervisor privately.

Confidentiality

Issues discussed during peer support are confidential within the parameters specified by law, department policy, and clinical supervision. Safeguarding acquired information is a primary obligation of team members. Subject to the limitations of law, information received in confidence shall not be revealed without the express consent of the person involved. Express consent to reveal information constitutes a waiver of confidentiality. In cases where express consent is granted, information will be provided only to those specifically designated to receive the information.

The statutory privilege for peer support team member confidentiality is specified in C.R.S. 13-90-107(m), *Who may not testify without consent.*

Team members must advise all persons with whom they interact in a peer support role of the limitations of peer support team member confidentiality. This includes that the information discussed will be communicated to the clinical supervisor.

In the event that information received in a peer support interaction must be revealed by mandate of law, PST members shall reveal such information only after an effort to elicit the person's voluntary disclosure has failed. In cases where it is appropriate, the peer support team member should inform the person of the obligatory actions necessary. Information revealed under such circumstances shall be provided only to the appropriate persons and public authorities.

In the unlikely event that a PST member receives information during a peer support interaction that there is a viable threat of harm or violence toward another person or persons, a *duty to warn* exists. This information is not confidential. The PST member must warn the threatened person(s), contact the team coordinator or clinical supervisor immediately, and take any other actions deemed appropriate for the circumstances.

PST Scheduled Meetings

Attending scheduled PST meetings is a primary obligation of PST members. The Peer Support Team meets monthly to allow for clinical supervision, on-going training, and team cohesion. If a team member is unable to attend a meeting, he or she should:

1. notify the team coordinator or an assistant team coordinator in advance of the meeting when possible or contact the team coordinator or an assistant team coordinator as soon as practical after the scheduled meeting,
2. obtain a copy of any training materials presented at the meeting, and
3. schedule an individual supervision meeting or otherwise contact the clinical supervisor if he or she has engaged in any PST interactions since the previous supervisory contact.

Excessive absences from the PST monthly meetings and training will be addressed by the team coordinator, assistant coordinators, and the clinical supervisor on an individual basis. Continued excessive absences may result in the team member's removal from the PST.

V. Duty to Take Action

Peace officer members of the PST are required to make an arrest in cases where there is probable cause that a crime has been committed within a domestic relationship. Peace officer members and other PST members who are mandatory reporters must also take action in cases of actual or suspected child abuse or neglect, and in cases of at-risk elder abuse or exploitation.

VI. Clarification of Peer Support Interactions

Peer Support Team members are responsible for clarifying the role in which they are functioning when interacting with others. Peer Support Team members must remain aware of potential conflicts of interest when providing peer support to individuals with whom they work or directly or indirectly supervise.

VII. Availability for Call-out

The Peer Support Team will provide Dispatch with a list of team members. In the event that PST support is requested through Dispatch, Dispatch will contact the team coordinator. If the team coordinator is unavailable, an assistant coordinator will be contacted. The coordinator or assistant coordinator contacted will assess the circumstances and arrange for appropriate PST response and intervention.

In the event that the PST coordinator and assistant coordinators cannot be contacted, Dispatch will continue to call team members in the order listed in Dispatch until a team member is contacted. The team member contacted will then act as coordinator. This team member will assess the circumstances and arrange for appropriate PST response and intervention.

VIII. Compensation

Peer Support Team members do not maintain a paid on-call status. Therefore, PST members are not eligible for on-call compensation. Peer Support Team members who are called out or otherwise function in their PST capacity during off-duty hours will be compensated as specified in department policy.

IX. Debriefing and Debriefing Process

PST members may facilitate debriefings when appropriate. All PST debriefings must be approved by the clinical supervisor. Approval is required because of research which suggests that debriefing participants may be retraumatized or vicariously traumatized during the debriefing process. Prior to the start of PST debriefings the "Limits of Confidentiality: Debriefing Statement for Peer

Support Team Members" must be read. Debriefing attendance is voluntary.

Various debriefing protocols may be utilized depending upon the actual circumstances. Team members recognize that the debriefing process is dynamic. Peer Support Team members remain flexible and facilitate debriefings in a manner that best meets the perceived needs of participants.

Peer Support Team members may invite persons not directly involved in the incident to attend a debriefing if it is thought that they can positively contribute to or benefit from the debriefing process. All such invitations must be approved by the clinical supervisor, team coordinator, or an assistant coordinator.

Debriefing participants may be accompanied by personal support persons. Personal support persons may attend debriefings if their participation is not prohibited by other sections of these operational guidelines.

X. Media

Media representatives are prohibited from attending debriefings. Any PST information released to the media will be accomplished as specified in department policy.

XI. Attorneys

Personal attorneys are prohibited from attending debriefings. This restriction is not intended to deprive any participant of legal representation. However, it is thought that the presence of a personal attorney inhibits the group process. Debriefing participants are encouraged to communicate to their attorneys that participation in an incident debriefing is voluntary and that debriefings facilitated by licensed mental health professionals are confidential within the limits prescribed by law.

XII. Other Agencies

The PST may be utilized to assist other agencies. The PST provides such assistance as specified by mutual aid policies.

XIII. Team Actions

Peer Support Team administrative concerns shall be discussed and decided at scheduled monthly meetings. Decisions or actions required by exigent circumstances may be made, implemented, or otherwise carried out by the clinical supervisor, team coordinator, an assistant coordinator, or acting coordinator.

XIV. Referral to Professional Counseling Services

Peer Support Team members may find it appropriate to inform those involved in peer support of available options for additional counseling. Available options include the department psychologist, Employee Assistance Program counselors, community private practitioners, self-help groups, and the various helping agencies within the community. It may also be appropriate to refer a person to specialized resources including but not limited to attorneys and financial advisors.

XV. Reach Out

Peer Support Team members may initiate a reach out. In a reach out, a PST member initiates supportive contact with a person who has been exposed to a critical incident, a life-circumstance change, cumulative stressors, or other known or suspected stressor.

XVI. Leave of Absence

Peer Support Team members may request a leave of absence from the PST for up to one year. A request for a leave of absence must be submitted in writing to the team coordinator. If the team coordinator wishes to request a leave of absence, the request must be submitted to the clinical supervisor. Any request for a leave of absence must specify the length of absence requested and the date of anticipated return to active status. During a leave of absence the PST member may attend monthly or otherwise scheduled PST training.

XVII. Resignation from the Team

Peer Support Team members may resign from the team by submitting a written resignation to the team coordinator. Any team member considering resignation must be certain that all ongoing peer support interactions are appropriately terminated, referred to other team members or the clinical supervisor, or referred to professional counseling resources.

XVIII. Removal from the Team

"All members of the PST serve at the discretion of the chief of police" (Policy Directive XXX-XX).

The chief of police may remove any team member from the Peer Support Team. The team coordinator in consultation with the clinical supervisor may request that the chief of police remove from the Peer Support Team any member who has been determined to have acted in violation of law, departmental policy, or the PST operational guidelines. Such a request may also be presented when a team member has been determined to have acted in a manner that undermines the credibility or fundamental ethical principles of the Peer Support Team.

XIX. Compliance with the Peer Support Team Operational Guidelines

Peer Support Team members are required by policy to function in compliance with the Peer Support Team Operational Guidelines:

The peer support team operates within the parameters set forth in the department approved Peer Support Team Operational Guidelines. (Policy XXX-XX, paragraph XX).

APPENDIX D

Foundation Building Blocks of Functional Relationships

Functional relationships are characterized by a balance between each person's relationship rights and relationship responsibilities. This balance is best achieved by maintaining a solid relationship foundation. This is true not only of marriages and other romantic relationships, but of all relationships.

The Foundation Building Blocks of Functional Relationships describes the primary components of functional relationships. The stronger each block, the more functional the relationship.

Foundation Building Blocks of Functional Relationships

1. *Emotional connection.* All relationships are characterized by feelings or the emotional connections that exist between or among relationship members. Feelings frequently alter or influence perceptions and behaviors. Love is a common emotional connection. The emotional connection established between persons can alter, or be altered by, any or all of the other blocks.

2. *Trust.* Trust is a fundamental building block of all functional relationships. Trust is related to many other components of

functional relationships including fidelity, dependability, and honesty.

3. *Honesty.* Functional relationships are characterized by a high degree of caring honesty. There is a place for not hurting others feelings and not addressing every issue. However, consistent misrepresentation or avoidance to avoid short-term conflict often results in the establishment of negative outcomes such as long-term resentment and invalidation.

4. *Assumption of honesty.* With trust, we can assume honesty in others. A relationship in which honesty cannot be assumed is plagued with suspicion. Such relationships are characterized by trying to mind-read the "real" meaning of various interactions.

5. *Respect.* Respect is demonstrated in all areas of functional relationships—verbal communication, nonverbal behaviors, openness for discussion, conflict resolution, and so on. Without respect, relationships cannot remain functional and problem resolution communication is not possible.

6. *Tolerance.* The acceptance of personal differences and individual preferences are vital to keeping relationships working well. A degree of mutual tolerance makes forgiveness possible and relationships more pleasant. It also reduces points of conflict.

7. *Responsiveness.* Your responsiveness to others helps to validate their importance to you. It reflects your commitment and demonstrates relationship meaningfulness. Responsiveness is especially important in families and in hierarchical work relationships.

8. *Flexibility.* Personal rigidity frequently strains relationships and limits potential functional boundaries. Highly functional relationships are characterized by reasonable flexibility so

that when stressed, they bend without breaking. Many things are not as serious as they first seem. Develop and maintain a sense of humor as part of flexibility.

9. *Communication.* Make it safe for communication. Speak and listen in a calm manner. Allow others to express thoughts and feelings without interruption. Stay mindful of the difference between *hearing* and *listening.* Safe and functional communication is characterized by listening.

10. *Commitm*ent. Long term functional relationships are characterized by commitment and a willingness to work on problems. This is accomplished by acceptance of personal responsibility, attempts to see things from other perspectives, conflict resolution, and the ability to repair and move beyond perceived transgressions.

Foundation reinforcers of functional relationships: (1) the assumption of good faith in your partner and (2) the absence of intentional harm.

In troubled marriages the fundamental blocks of the relationship foundation have been damaged. Because the blocks are the foundation upon which the marriage is built, the damage in the foundation is reflected in the relationship. The couple will experience a degree of marital discord commensurate to the foundation damage. Most persons in troubled marriages do not seek help until marital dysfunction reaches some crisis. By this time, the foundation may have sustained too much damage for the relationship to be successfully repaired.

Special Status

All of us have *special status* people. Spouses, significant others, partners, and so on are special status people. They are the only persons in the universe that hold this unique status in our lives. It is ok to do some things differently for those with special status... for instance, yielding in an argument. Doing this for special status persons increases the likelihood that they will return the favor. For special status persons and others, model the behavior that you wish in return. A useful way to remember this is, *you often get what you give.*

APPENDIX E

Diagnostic Criteria for Posttraumatic Stress Disorder

Criterion A: stressor

The person was exposed to: death, threatened death, actual or threatened serious injury, or actual or threatened sexual violence, as follows: (one required)

1. Direct exposure.
2. Witnessing, in person.
3. Indirectly, by learning that a close relative or close friend was exposed to trauma. If the event involved actual or threatened death, it must have been violent or accidental.
4. Repeated or extreme indirect exposure to aversive details of the event(s), usually in the course of professional duties (e.g., first responders, collecting body parts; professionals repeatedly exposed to details of child abuse). This does not include indirect non-professional exposure through electronic media, television, movies, or pictures.

Criterion B: intrusion symptoms

The traumatic event is persistently re-experienced in the following way(s): (one required)

1. Recurrent, involuntary, and intrusive memories. Note: Children older than six may express this symptom in repetitive play.
2. Traumatic nightmares. Note: Children may have frightening dreams without content related to the trauma(s).
3. Dissociative reactions (e.g., flashbacks) which may occur on a continuum from brief episodes to complete loss of consciousness. Note: Children may reenact the event in play.
4. Intense or prolonged distress after exposure to traumatic reminders. Marked physiologic reactivity after exposure to trauma-related stimuli.

Criterion C: avoidance

Persistent effortful avoidance of distressing trauma-related stimuli after the event: (one required)

1. Trauma-related thoughts or feelings.
2. Trauma-related external reminders (e.g., people, places, conversations, activities, objects, or situations).

Criterion D: negative alterations in cognitions and mood

Negative alterations in cognitions and mood that began or worsened after the traumatic event: (two required)

1. Inability to recall key features of the traumatic event (usually dissociative amnesia; not due to head injury, alcohol, or drugs).
2. Persistent (and often distorted) negative beliefs and expectations about oneself or the world (e.g., "I am bad," "The world is completely dangerous").
3. Persistent distorted blame of self or others for causing the traumatic event or for resulting consequences.
4. Persistent negative trauma-related emotions (e.g., fear, horror, anger, guilt, or shame).

5. Markedly diminished interest in (pre-traumatic) significant activities.
6. Feeling alienated from others (e.g., detachment or estrangement).
7. Constricted affect: persistent inability to experience positive emotions.

Criterion E: alterations in arousal and reactivity

Trauma-related alterations in arousal and reactivity that began or worsened after the traumatic event: (two required)

1. Irritable or aggressive behavior
2. Self-destructive or reckless behavior
3. Hypervigilance
4. Exaggerated startle response
5. Problems in concentration
6. Sleep disturbance

Criterion F: duration

Persistence of symptoms (in Criteria B, C, D, and E) for more than one month

Criterion G: functional significance

Significant symptom-related distress or functional impairment (e.g., social, occupational).

Criterion H: exclusion

Disturbance is not due to medication, substance use, or other illness.

Specify if: With dissociative symptoms.

In addition to meeting criteria for diagnosis, an individual experiences high levels of either of the following in reaction to trauma-related stimuli:

a. Depersonalization: experience of being an outside observer of or detached from oneself (e.g., feeling as if "this is not happening to me" or one were in a dream).
b. Derealization: experience of unreality, distance, or distortion (e.g., "things are not real").

Specify if: With delayed expression.

Full diagnosis is not met until at least six months after the trauma(s), although onset of symptoms may occur immediately.

From: American Psychiatric Association. (2013) *Diagnostic and statistical manual of mental disorders*, (5th ed.). Washington, DC: Author.

APPENDIX F

Critical Incident Management and the Trauma Intervention Program

Critical Incident Management

Concept of *second injury* - second injury occurs when an officer is treated poorly following a critical incident, even if unintentionally. Second injury is especially likely if the poor treatment comes from the officer's department. Remember, you don't have to intend harm to do harm.

1. Remove officer from scene/controlled environment/away from suspect's family/not isolated/gatekeeper and peer support (See *Officer-Involved Incident Protocol*)
    Officer notification of spouse and family/notification as set by policy if incapacitated
    On-scene support (peer support team, psychologist)/ confidentiality
    Contact from top administrator (chief or sheriff). *Ongoing* admin/staff support
    Replacement of weapon (if taken as evidence) with like weapon/return of badge if clothing is taken and badge is not evidence/replacement badge if badge is taken as evidence
    Issues of officer blood or breath sample – voluntary, probable cause, or policy
    Police vehicle considerations if vehicle is assigned

Administrative leave pending processing of incident/press releases/telephone, email screening/officer and officer's family security

2. Recognition of personal risk – recognition of officer's perceptions, conceptions, emotions, effort, and actions – appoint department contact officer. Attorney for officer if requested without negative consequences for officer. Clear distinction between criminal and administrative investigation: Miranda advisement? Garrity advisement?

3. Family involvement: spouse/children (immediate support, security, nature of incident, issues of vulnerability, peer reactions, work, school, released press information, extended family responses, etc). Prepare for possible negativity: press, segments of community, family members of suspect, other sources.

4. Debriefing if appropriate, other support interventions if debriefing is unwarranted. Debriefing: voluntary, invitation of participants – consider support persons, dispatch personnel, other agency personnel/individual follow-up/peer support team member reach-out, timeframe (see *Guidelines for Conducting a Police Critical Incident Debriefing* and *Peer Support Team and Debriefing Issues*).

5. Expedite criminal and administrative investigations, district attorney, review boards, etc - expedite closure for involved officers.

6. Consider scheduled court hearings and assigned off-duty work/evaluated on an individual case basis – Consider any other incident-specific factors.

Trauma Intervention Program

The Trauma Intervention Program (TIP) is a critical incident protocol guide for police agencies. It consists of several recommended components and strategies designed to assist officers and their families with the physical, emotional, and psychological aftermath of a critical incident.

The Trauma Intervention Program works best for officers when certain precursors have been completed. These are: (1) comprehensive pre-hire psychological assessment, (2) stress inoculation and trauma management training in the pre-service skills academy, (3) participation in the PATROL program during field training, and (4) involvement of spouse/family in agency familiarization and specialized education.

The Trauma Intervention Program: (1) has some elements that are implemented simultaneously and some elements that are implemented sequentially, (2) is flexible and may be modified to meet the needs of any agency, (3) may be modified to fit within available resources, (4) incorporates a police psychologist and a properly supervised peer support team, and (5) may be adjusted to accommodate circumstances wherein the involved officer was injured.

The Trauma Intervention Program is presented in outline form with elaborative information in italics.

> Precursor Programs—Pre-hire psychological assessment, pre-service skills academy orientation and training, PATROL, and spouse/family education.

> 1. *On-scene support*—provided by the police psychologist and the peer support team. *On-scene support begins with the police psychologist and/or selected members of the peer support team. The officer becomes the client of the police psychologist so that confidentiality privileges are established.*

2. *Critical incident debriefing or small group/individual intervention*—as needed, provided by the police psychologist and peer support team. *Debriefings are best utilized for critical incidents where a need for debriefing has been identified. Often, individual interactions or small group interventions are adequate. The appropriate interventions are decided upon by the police psychologist with input from the peer support team. Members of the peer support team play a significant role in this part of the TIP. Officer participation in any group intervention is voluntary.*

3. *Considerations for intervention*—police psychologist. *The police psychologist initiates a counseling support program and continues to work with the officer and family. The following represent some of the issues which are considered. (Adjusted if the officer has been injured or is hospitalized):*

   - obtain contact numbers
   - criminal and administrative investigation issues
   - officer and officer's family security
   - spouse/children/family considerations
   - history—background and current status (bio-psycho-social)
   - medical, medications, psychological, social-support
   - support interventions: assessment and implementation
   - supportive therapy (cognitive/emotional/EMDR)
   - mental wellness – continued assessment
   - memory—stress response and frequent outcome
   - photographs and recordings—as appropriate
   - reports—review as needed
   - educational and informative material—as appropriate

4. *Current work status: administrative leave or other*—modified work status in accordance with policy. *The police psychologist works with agency administrators to ensure that an agency contact person is appointed, that agency support continues,*

that any obligations that existed prior to the incident are managed in a satisfactory manner, and that the officer is not further traumatized.

- department contact person
- *ongoing* department support
- administrators, supervisors, and peers
- officer and family security
- court, training, meetings, and so on
- police vehicle and equipment
- modified-duty considerations

5. *Equipment and other stimulus reintroduction if necessary*— anxiety triggers (uniform, patrol vehicle, radio traffic, etc). *This component of the TIP is unnecessary in some cases and absolutely necessary in others. Much depends upon whether there has been an acquired undesirable conditioned response to a previously neutral stimulus.*

6. *Incident site visit*—visit to location of incident from a psychological perspective. *Although the officer may have returned to the location of the incident for investigative purposes, this is insufficient to accomplish what is intended in the TIP site visit. TIP site visits are informative, experiential, sometimes emotional, and are used to help the officer further process the incident. They are also used to rule out the presence of anxiety triggers and other conditioned responses.*

7. *Firing range*—shooting exposure for shooting incidents (non-qualification, qualification). *If the critical incident involved the use of an officer's firearm, prior to returning to work, the officer shoots a non-qualifying course of fire for exposure (can be a loaner weapon). This is to ascertain whether the officer has any difficulties handling a firearm post-incident. The timing of this exposure is critical to the officer's recovery and is to be determined by the police psychologist. Later, prior to returning to duty, the officer shoots a qualifying*

course of fire. If the actual firearm used in the incident was taken for evidence, the officer shoots a qualifying course with the weapon once it is returned. The psychologist or a peer support team member may accompany the officer if requested or otherwise assessed appropriate.

8. *Officer Wellness Assessment*—as a component of the psychologist's support intervention (clinical interview, mental status examination, symptom assessment, rule out clinically significant incident-related distress or impairment). *The OWA is utilized to: (1) determine if the incident generated a stressor-related disorder that would prevent the officer from safely returning to duty, (2) determine if the incident exacerbated a pre-existing condition that would prevent the officer from safely returning to duty, and (3) help determine optimal timing for the initiation of graded reentry.*

9. *Graded reentry*—return-to-duty protocol (RTD). *Graded reentry allows the involved officer to work with a partner and gradually resume the responsibilities of solo duty.*

10. *Additional involvement of peer support team*—as needed. *The need for continued support from the peer support team is assessed and provided as requested or deemed appropriate.*

11. *Other considerations*—specific to the officer and incident. *This component of the TIP assesses, acknowledges, and addresses issues specific to the officer. Other persons or agencies may become involved if needed to address specific issues.*

12. *Follow through for the year of firsts*—first birthday, Christmas, and other meaningful dates, since the incident. *A member of the peer support team is chosen by the officer to provide support throughout the first year. This PST member helps the officer process any issues that might arise on holidays, the anniversary date of the incident, or any other date significant to the officer.*

Appendix G

Suggestions for Supporting Officers Involved in Shootings and Other Trauma

The following suggestions were written by Alexis Artwohl and published in her book, DEADLY FORCE ENCOUNTERS, co-authored by Loren Christensen (1997) (reprinted with permission). The thoughts and comments of Jack A. Digliani are represented in italics (added with permission).

1. Do initiate contact in the form of a phone call or note to let a traumatized officer know you are concerned and available for support or help (don't forget to acknowledge their significant others). In the case of a shooting, remember that the non-shooters who were at the scene are just as likely to be affected by the incident as the shooters. Remember that there are many other events besides shootings that traumatize cops. When in doubt, call. *Do not fall into the trap that "others will do it, so I don't have to." Your expression of support will be appreciated.*

2. Offer to stay with a traumatized officer/friend for the first day or two after the event if you know they live alone (or help find a mutual friend who can). Alternatively, you could offer for the officer to stay with you and your family. *This type of support for an officer living alone can be quite beneficial for the first few days following a traumatic incident.*

3. Let the traumatized officer decide how much contact he/
    she wants to have with you. They may be overwhelmed with
    phone calls and it may take a while for them to return your call.
    Also, they and their family may want some "down time" with
    minimal interruptions. *The police psychologist, a member
    of the peer support team (PST), a trusted friend, or other
    designated person can be asked to communicate a request
    for down time if involved officers need a communication
    hiatus.*

4. Don't ask for an account of the shooting, but let the
    traumatized officer know you are willing to listen to whatever
    they want to talk about. Officers may get tired of repeating
    the story and find "curiosity seekers" distasteful. Be mindful
    that there is usually no legally privileged confidentiality for
    peer discussions. *You can let involved officers know that
    you are there for them without being intrusive. Do not
    be offended if the officer does not want to talk about the
    incident, regardless of your previous relationship. Members
    of police peer support teams that meet specified criteria
    are protected from testifying without consent in Colorado
    under C.R.S. 13-90-107(m), however this protection does
    not extend to criminal matters. A privileged communication
    relationship exists between officers and various others
    including psychologists, attorneys, licensed or ordained
    clergy members, spouses, physicians, and other licensed or
    supervised mental health professionals. PST members and
    others must make all disclosures mandated by law.*

5. Ask questions that show support and acceptance such as,
    "Is there anything I can do to help you or your family?" *In
    some cases where the pre-existing relationship will support
    it, just doing instead of asking is appropriate.*

6. Accept their reaction as normal for them and avoid suggesting
    how they "should" be feeling. Officers have a wide range
    of reactions to traumatic events. *If part of their reaction*

is thoughts or feelings of homicide or suicide, or should you observe behaviors consistent with the serious mental illness (especially depression), you should contact the police psychologist or the PST immediately.

7.   Remember that the key to helping a traumatized officer is nonjudgmental listening. *Just listening without trying to solve a problem or imposing your views can go a long way to helping the involved officer.*

8.   Don't say, "I understand how you feel" unless you have been through the same experience. Do feel free to offer a BRIEF sharing of a similar experience you might have had to help them know they are not alone in how they feel. However, this is not the time to work on your own trauma issues with this person. If your friend's event triggers some of your own emotions, find someone else to talk to who can offer support to you. *It's worthwhile to keep in mind that individual officers will frequently perceive a critical incident in a somewhat unique way. However, there is enough overlap in our experiences to allow us to relate to some degree to the experience of involved officers. A good rule to follow: If the involved officer asks you a question about your experience or how you handled a past incident, respond fully to the question, then re-focus on the officer. If additional questions are asked, respond in a similar fashion...the officer is requesting more information from you. Your responses are likely to normalize feelings, thoughts, and behaviors which may be new or strange to the officer. Keep your responses concise and talk in plain language. Do not get stuck in your own unresolved issues. <u>The last thing an officer who has experienced a traumatic incident needs is to become your therapist</u>.*

9.   Don't encourage the use of alcohol. It is best for officers to avoid all use of alcohol for a few weeks so they can process what has happened to them with a clear head and true

feelings uncontaminated by drug use. *Remember, alcohol is a behavioral disinhibitor in small dosages and a central nervous system depressant in larger quantities. It is best not to be affected in either of these ways when attempting to process a traumatic event. Additionally, in order to avoid over stimulation and symptoms of withdrawal, caffeine intake should remain close to normal. Caffeine is a diuretic and vasoconstrictor. Its stimulant properties increase autonomic arousal and can cause a jittery feeling. Even small amounts of caffeine can interfere with sleep onset and maintenance in those not accustomed to it. Officers should stay within their normal limits of caffeine consumption.*

10. Don't "congratulate" officers after shootings or call them names like "terminator" or otherwise joke around about the incident. Officers often have mixed feelings about deadly force encounters and find such comments offensive. *Some of this may be due to feelings of elation that the officer survived the incident and performed well, while at the same time realizing that he or she had to injure or kill another person in order to survive. Mixed feelings, along with a heightened sense of danger, are two of the most common after-effects of shooting incidents. Mixed feelings are common in cases of "suicide by cop," wherein the suspect displayed a toy or replica firearm with the goal of being killed by the police.*

11. Offer positive statements about the officers themselves, such as, "I'm glad you're O.K." *Critical incidents frequently bring forward emotions and thoughts not present in everyday living. Making positive statements demonstrates support and caring. This frequently helps officers deal with the issues inherent in critical and traumatic experiences.*

12. You are likely to find yourself second-guessing the shooting, but keep your comments to yourself. Critical comments have a way of coming back to the involved officer and it only does harm to the officer who is probably second-guessing

him/herself and struggling to recover. Besides, most of the second-guessing is wrong anyway. *Second-guessing largely involves evaluating a decision at a particular time with information that became known after the decision had to be made. Keep in mind that the best anyone can do is to make reasonable decisions based upon the information available at the time the decision had to be made. Every cop, every day, makes decisions based on limited information.*

13. Encourage the officers to take care of themselves. Show support for such things as taking as much time off as they need to recover. Also encourage the officer to participate in debriefings and counseling. *Officers involved in shootings and other serious critical incidents are engaged in support programs, counseling, and debriefings as specified by department policy. Remember, employees may, at any time, seek confidential assistance from the police psychologist, the PST, or the Employee Assistance Program for any intensity event or ongoing stressor.*

14. Gently confront them about negative behavioral and emotional changes you notice that persist for longer than one month. Encourage them to seek professional help. *A general rule of confrontation: confront to the degree that the underlying relationship will support. In other words, if done in a caring way, the closer you feel to a person, the more you can confront without jeopardizing the relationship.*

15. Don't refer to officers who are having emotional problems as "mentals" or other derogatory terms. Stigmatizing each other encourages officers to deny their psychological injuries and not to get the help they need. *Getting through critical incidents is hard enough. We do not need to make it more difficult on each other by derogatory labeling. This includes general attitudes communicated in everyday speech as well as specific comments following a particular event. Do not reinforce or contribute to the secondary danger of policing.*

16. Educate yourself about trauma reactions by reviewing written materials or consulting with someone who has familiarity with this topic. *The police psychologist and PST have several handouts and other material which can assist you in learning more about critical incidents, trauma, and traumatic responses. Contact any member of the PST to obtain this information (Law Enforcement Critical Incident Handbook).*

17. Officers want to return to normality as soon as possible. Don't pretend like the event didn't happen but do treat the traumatized officers like you always have. Don't avoid them, treat them as fragile, or otherwise drastically change your behavior with them. *It is normal for officers who have been through a traumatic experience to become a bit more sensitive to how others act toward them. This increased sensitivity is usually temporary. You can help involved officers work through this sensitivity as well as larger aspects of the incident by just being yourself.*

18. Remember that in this case, your mother was right: If you don't have anything nice to say, don't say anything at all". *In the final analysis, we cannot know which side of a critical incident we will find ourselves - an officer looking to others for support or an officer attempting to provide support. In policing, confronting circumstances that have the potential to traumatize is more common than in many other professions. Our strength and defense lies in how we treat each other.*

APPENDIX H

25 Suggestions and Considerations for Officers Involved in a Critical Incident

1. The incident is over. You're safe. No matter what type of critical incident you have experienced, do not forget that you are now safe.

2. Realize that your survival instinct was an asset at the time of the incident and that it remains intact to assist you now and in the future if needed.

3. Emotions following a critical incident are normally different or more intense than usual. This is due to the nature and intensity of critical incidents. Accept your emotions as normal and part of the incident survival and recovery process.

4. Accept that you may have experienced fear. Fear is a normal emotion and should not be interpreted as weakness.

5. Learn about or become acquainted with the features of normal post-critical incident responses. This will help you to understand that much of what you're feeling is a normal part of the recovery process.

6. Accept that you cannot always control events, but you can control or at least influence your responses. If you are

troubled by a perceived lack of control, focus on the fact that you had *some* control during the event. You used your strength to respond in a certain way.

7. Talk to someone. Discuss your experiences and feelings with someone you trust. Seek a person with privileged confidentiality communication protections if necessary.

8. Try not to second-guess your actions. Evaluate your actions based on your perceptions at the time of the event, not afterwards. Remember that *every cop, every day* has to make decisions based upon limited and sometimes faulty information. It is imperative to keep this in mind following a critical incident.

9. Understand that your actions during the incident were based on the need to make critical decisions for action. Some of these decisions had to be made within seconds.

10. Accept that your behavior was appropriate to your perceptions and feelings at the time of the incident. No one is perfect. It's normal to like and dislike some of your actions during and following a critical incident.

11. Focus on the things you did that you feel good about. Positive outcomes are often produced by less than ideal (especially in retrospect) actions.

12. Following a critical incident, officers are often more critical of themselves than they would be of other officers in identical circumstances. Do not become your own worst critic. Talk to yourself in the same way you would to another officer.

13. It is normal to have the incident play over and over in your head. Repetitive incident replay is a feature of the psychological process leading to recovery. Incident replay normally gradually subsides over a period of several weeks.

You will notice a decline in the frequency, intensity, and duration of incident-replay over time.

14. Take some time for yourself if needed but avoid isolating yourself physically and emotionally from your family and others that care about you. Avoiding isolation may be especially difficult if you are feeling numb or emotionally "flat". Do your best to positively and progressively positively engage others. The numb feeling, if present, will gradually subside.

15. Prepare yourself for some negativity. There are few police critical incidents that are not criticized by someone, especially if you had to shoot to defend yourself. No matter how necessary the use of lethal force was, it seems that there is at least one person who will say things like, "They didn't have to shoot him", "These cops are out of control", or "He (the suspect) would not have hurt anybody, the cops overreacted". You must *stay grounded in what you know to be true* to minimize the damaging effects of unjustified and uninformed private or public opinion.

16. Some people will force police officers to shoot them. If your critical incident was a *suicide by cop*, it is natural to experience a broad range of emotion. These can vary from feeling sorry for the person to intense anger for involving you in their wish to die. It is also possible to experience several, seemingly contradictory emotions in reference to the suicidal person. Do not forget that he or she removed all your other options and you had to defend yourself from their potentially lethal behavior.

17. Sleeping can be difficult for awhile, and you may have unusual dreams during the time that you are sleeping. This is normal. Unusual sleep and dreaming patterns, if present, usually return to normal within a few weeks.

18. Avoid using alcohol as a primary critical incident stress management strategy. Although alcohol might "relax" you and help you to fall asleep if you're having trouble sleeping, it will not help you to maintain restful sleep and it is not a good relaxation strategy.

19. Maintain your exercise routine. If you do not have a routine, start some daily light exercise. Walking is excellent. Even mild exercise or other physical activity helps to dissipate stress and aids in sleep onset and maintenance.

20. Keep caffeine consumption within your normal limits. It's ok to lessen caffeine consumption for a few days, especially if you're having difficulty sleeping. Abrupt cessation of all caffeine by those accustomed to consuming caffeine will cause symptoms of caffeine withdrawal.

21. Do not take the activities of the "system" personally. Keep the needs of the various systems (police department, DA's office, administrative investigation, criminal investigation, the press, etc) in perspective. In terms of the investigations, *remember that an officer's best defense against false accusations is a thorough and complete incident investigation.*

22. Try to be patient. Do this on two levels: (1) be patient with yourself - it takes time to psychologically work through a critical incident, and (2) be patient with everyone and everything else – your spouse, your department, incident investigators, the DA's office, etc. Even though you will want some things completed swiftly, most things will take more time than desired.

23. Assume responsibility for your positive recovery. Many police departments have professional and peer support protocols in place to assist officers involved in critical incidents, but many do not. Do not hesitate asking for the help you need. Do not become a victim of the secondary danger of policing.

24. Be especially aware of any personal suicidal thoughts or feelings. Although rare, suicidal thoughts have been known to occur in officers following critical incidents. Keep yourself safe. If you are having suicidal thoughts, contact a responsible person immediately. Remain open to appropriate support and intervention. Suicidal thoughts following a critical incident are normally of short duration and respond well to even the mildest modes of support.

25. Do not allow the incident to damage you, your family, or your career. Take care of your family and let them take care of you. (see *Officers and Spouses: Critical Incident Information* in the Law Enforcement Critical Incident Handbook). Take advantage of available support resources.

> Remember, police critical incidents happen because you are a police officer and there are circumstances beyond your control, not because of who you are as a person.

Positive Recovery

Keep in mind that you are naturally resilient. If you do not feel good now, allow yourself some time to process the event. You will feel better over time. Resiliency and positive recovery involves the following:

1. Accepting what happened. You will accept any experience of fear and any feelings of vulnerability as part of being human. Vulnerability is not helplessness.

2. Accepting that no one can control everything. You will focus on your behaviors and the appropriate application of authority. You will keep a positive perspective.

3. You will learn and grow from the experience. You will be able to assess all future circumstances on their own merits. You will become stronger and smarter.

4. You will include survivorship into your life perspective. You may re-evaluate life's goals, priorities, and meaning. You will gain wisdom from your survivorship.

5. You will be aware of changes in yourself that may contribute to problems at home, work, and other environments. You will know how to dissipate undesirable reactive emotion. You will work positively to manage or overcome these issues.

6. You will increase the intimacy of your actions and communications with those you love. You will remain open to the feedback and care of those who love you.

Getting Help

No one can work through the aftermath of a critical incident for you, but you do not have to go it alone. Keep an open mind. Allow your family, friends, and peers to help.

Seek professional assistance if you get stuck, if you do not "feel like yourself" or if your friends or family notice dysfunctional emotional responses or behavior. Do not ignore those who care about you. Stay connected to your loved ones.

This page adapts and includes information from the *Colorado Law Enforcement Academy Handbook* and *Reflections of a Police Psychologist* (2nd ed) (Digliani, J.A., 2015).

APPENDIX I

Peer Support Team Limits of Confidentiality Pocket Card

(State of Colorado)

Police Department Peer Support Team
Limitations of Confidentiality

The confidentiality privileges of law enforcement peer support team members is specified in C.R.S. 13-90-107(m).

Peace officer PST members are required to take action, including arrest, in domestic violence cases where probable cause exists that a crime has been committed (C.R.S. 18-6-803.6)

Information:

Information will be brought under supervision with the PST clinical supervisor as required by peer support team policy and operational guidelines.

There are no confidentiality privileges for peer support team members in the federal court system.

Information is not confidential when:

- A PST member is witness or party to an incident which prompted the delivery of peer support services. C.R.S. 13-90-107 (m).
- Information received indicates actual or suspected child abuse or neglect (C.R.S. 19-3-304) or actual or suspected abuse or exploitation of an at-risk elder (C.R.S. 18-6.5-108).
- Due to drug or alcohol intoxication the person is a clear and immediate danger to self or others (C.R.S. 27-81-111 and C.R.S. 27-82-107).
- There is reason to believe that the person has a mental illness, and due to the mental illness, is an imminent threat to self or others; or is gravely disabled (C.R.S. 27-65-102).
- There is information indicative of any criminal conduct. (C.R.S. 13-90-107 (m)).

Appendix J

12 Irrational Ideas of Rational-Emotive Behavior Therapy

(and their rational counterparts) – Albert Ellis

1. The idea that it is a dire necessity for adults to be loved by significant others for almost everything they do -- Instead of their concentrating on their own self-respect, on winning approval for practical purposes, and on loving rather than on being loved.

2. The idea that certain acts are awful or wicked, and that people who perform such acts should be severely damned -- Instead of the idea that certain acts are self-defeating or antisocial, and that people who perform such acts are behaving stupidly, ignorantly, or neurotically, and would be better helped to change. People's poor behaviors do not make them rotten individuals.

3. The idea that it is horrible when things are not the way we like them to be -- Instead of the idea that it is too bad, that we would better try to change or control bad conditions so that they become more satisfactory, and, if that is not possible, we had better temporarily accept and gracefully lump their existence.

4. The idea that human misery is invariably externally caused and is forced on us by outside people and events -- Instead of the idea that neurosis is largely caused by the view that we take of unfortunate conditions.

5. The idea that if something is or may be dangerous or fearsome we should be terribly upset and endlessly obsess about it-- Instead of the idea that one would better frankly face it and render it non-dangerous and, when that is not possible, accept the inevitable.

6. The idea that it is easier to avoid than to face life difficulties and self-responsibilities -- Instead of the idea that the so-called easy way is usually much harder in the long run.

7. The idea that we absolutely need something other or stronger or greater than ourself on which to rely -- Instead of the idea that it is better to take the risks of thinking and acting less dependently.

8. The idea that we should be thoroughly competent, intelligent, and achieving in all possible respects -- Instead of the idea that we would better do rather than always need to do well, and accept ourself as a quite imperfect creature, who has general human limitations and specific fallibilities.

9. The idea that because something once strongly affected our life, it should indefinitely affect it -- Instead of the idea that we can learn from our past experiences but not be overly-attached to or prejudiced by them.

10. The idea that we must have certain and perfect control over things -- Instead of the idea that the world is full of improbability and chance and that we can still enjoy life despite this.

11. The idea that human happiness can be achieved by inertia and inaction -- Instead of the idea that we tend to be happiest when we are vitally absorbed in creative pursuits, or when we are devoting ourselves to people or projects outside ourselves.

12. The idea that we have virtually no control over our emotions and that we cannot help feeling disturbed about things -- Instead of the idea that we have real control over our destructive emotions if we choose to work at changing the "musturbatory" hypotheses which we often employ to create them.

Appendix K

Helping a Person that is Suicidal

The following guidelines may be useful when trying to help a person that is suicidal.

1) Take all suicidal comments and behaviors seriously.

2) Initiate a conversation. Express your concern and willingness to help. Listen closely without being judgmental.

3) If the person is intoxicated, arrange for detoxification. If the person is known to have an ongoing alcohol or substance use problem, support and encourage the person to seek and engage appropriate treatment.

4) Be mindful of what you say because the person may be overly sensitive to your remarks, but you do not have to "walk on eggshells." Be yourself.

5) Remain calm: the person may express strong emotion. This will normally dissipate naturally. You may also be emotionally affected. Accept your emotions as a natural and normal part of your caring interaction.

6) Acknowledge the person's difficulties without minimization or overstatement. Do not joke about what is serious to the person.

7) Avoid trying to "cheer up" the person. Instead, focus on listening and supporting.

8) Avoid providing problem solutions or recommendations unless asked. Encourage the person to seek professional assistance if necessary. Maintain your personal boundaries.

9) Bring the issue of suicide into the open. Ask about the person's current thoughts and feelings about suicide.

10) Ask about past suicidal thoughts, feelings, and attempts.

11) Ask about the availability of lethal means for suicide. Easy access to firearms is especially dangerous.

12) Remove firearms and other lethal means of suicide if necessary. Control potentially lethal prescribed medications or street drugs if warranted.

13) Determine if there is a suicidal plan – the more detailed and complete the plan, the greater the suicidal risk.

14) Suicidal thoughts are often the result of depression. Talk to the person about depression and the fact that depression can be effectively treated. Assure the person that with appropriate treatment for depression, suicidal thoughts and the feeling of wanting to die will diminish. Help to provide *realistic hope.*

15) Do not hesitate to ask for help: (1) from the suicidal person; ask the person to cooperate with you and your efforts to assist, (2) from others if warranted; ask appropriate others to assist you in your efforts to help the suicidal person.

16) If the person is not imminently suicidal, spend some time talking, "provide an ear," and offer emotional support. Depending on the circumstances and your relationship, encourage, assist,

or insist that the person engage professional services. If warranted, arrange for the person to be with others 24/7 for continued support and to add an additional level of person-safety.

17) If you feel that the person is imminently suicidal do not leave him or her alone. Contact the police or other emergency resource. Do this even if the person objects. Keep in mind that if the person refuses voluntary intervention, emergency involuntary evaluation and treatment may be necessary.

18) If you feel that the person is somewhat suicidal but you do not feel competent to assess the level of suicidality, do not leave him or her alone. Contact the police or other available assessment and support resource. Do this even if the person objects. This is the best way to keep the person safe.

19) Do not keep a suicidal secret, even if requested to do so. If necessary, gently explain that you must share the information provided to you and that you must contact appropriate others.

20) Follow up as appropriate. Factors influencing appropriate follow up include the degree of suicidality, your history with the person, your current relationship with the person, the current circumstances, how much future involvement you are willing to have with the person, and anticipated future circumstances.

APPENDIX L

Comprehensive Model for Police Advanced Strategic Support (COMPASS)

Positive and supportive agency administrators - Positive organizational environment

Pre-hire psychological assessment independent of police staff psychologist

Agency commitment to *staff psychologist* and *peer support team* concepts

Early involvement of staff psychologist
  (1) Establishes psychologist/officer relationship
  (2) Breaks down "shrink" stereotype
  (3) Stigma reduction for seeking help

In-service recruit academy: staff psychologist presentations -stress inoculation, critical incident protocol, preparation for FTO program, PATROL, function of peer support team, role and responsibilities staff psychologist, and other relevant topics

Psychologist and Training/Recruit Officer Liaison (PATROL) program: Trainee officer meets with psychologist at least once per Field Training Officer (FTO) training phase. PATROL is independent of FTO training but coordinated with FTO program. Spouse invited. Spouse program. Training, work, and non-work issues. Confidential setting. PATROL is a preemptive and proactive psychological support program for officers-in-training and their families

Enhances psychologist/officer relationship, continues stigma reduction for seeking help

Police staff psychologist: provides (1) psychological services for employees and their families - couples counseling (2) training and clinical supervision of the Peer Support Team (3) support for PST members (4) critical incident protocol development, (5) coordination with other support resources, (6) liaison with other agencies, (7) Make it Safe Initiative, (8) other services as appropriate – *Employee Assistance Programs (EAP) and insurance plan community counseling services can be beneficial but appear insufficient to provide the range of support services optimal for police officers. The police psychologist is in a unique position to overcome the reluctance of many officers to seek professional support when needed*

Preemptive proactive programs – programs designed to assist officers prior to the development of difficulties – includes the PATROL program, the computer crimes child pornography investigators quarterly contact support program, Proactive Annual Check-In (PAC), and the TIP program.
In-service presentations (presented periodically) – stress inoculation, health and wellness, critical incident protocol and trauma intervention program, police marriage and family issues, interacting with special populations, officer suicide prevention, interacting with suicidal persons, and other relevant topics

Retirement preparation program – (1) Practical issues (financial, etc), (2) Psychological and emotional issues (3) Departing the police role, (4) Family and other social issues

Peer Support Team (PST): comprised of officers and others trained in peer support and functioning within written policy and operational guidelines:

(1) Structured with Coordinator, Clinical Advisor, or Clinical Supervisor

(2) Clinical supervision and "ladder of escalation" (referral, advisement, and immediate supervision when needed)

(3) Monthly in-service training and group supervision

(4) Integral part of staff psychologist pre-emptive and intervention programs

(5) *Major concepts* – interest, commitment, credibility, clinical supervision, confidentiality and limits, limitations of peer support, remaining within the boundaries of PST training, referral, special programs, and reach out

---

Peer Support Team Brochure, Peer Support Team Newsletter, PST shift briefing programs, PST debriefings – interventions, PST poster information

---

Spouse and family programs: specialized programs involving the PST and police psychologist designed to support the spouse and family members of police officers, couples and marriage enhancement programs and presentations

---

Police staff psychologist and peer support team members: the police psychologist and uninvolved members of the peer support team are made available to officers involved in *supervisory inquiries* and *internal investigations* – this information is specified within the officer-advisement investigative documents

---

Transitional adjustment support: when officers retire, resign, or are terminated they are eligible for three visits with the police psychologist beyond their employment

Retiree programs: programs for officers that retire from the department in good standing that offer volunteer opportunities, occasional or periodic social activities, and other meaningful continued involvement with the agency - recognition for years of service to the department and community

Officer and family

Health & Wellness

Police Officer Career

Professional and Peer Support

COMPASS - *Helping police officers to find their way*

APPENDIX M

Peer Support Team Code
of Ethical Conduct

As a member of an agency peer support team I am committed to the highest standards of peer support. I knowingly accept the responsibility associated with being a member of a peer support team.

Peer support team members:

1. engage in peer support within the parameters of their peer support training.
2. specify when they are functioning in their peer support role, and if uncertain whether an interaction is peer support, they inquire to clarify.
3. keep themselves current in all matters of peer support confidentially.
4. disclose peer support information only with appropriate consent, except in cases where allowed or mandated by law; and if uncertain whether disclosure is appropriate, consult with their clinical supervisor prior to disclosing information.
5. clearly specify the limits of peer support confidentiality prior to engaging in peer support.
6. remain aware of potential role conflicts and are especially vigilant to avoid role conflict if in a supervisory position.
7. make a reasonable effort to attend scheduled team meetings and programs of in-service training.

8. make referrals to other peer support team members, their clinical supervisor, and others when appropriate.
9. are careful providing peer support for persons with whom they have a troubled history. If the history cannot be overcome, they provide appropriate referral.
10. comply with peer support team statutes, policies, and operational guidelines.
11. do not utilize their peer support role for personal gain or advantage.
12. do not engage in inappropriate behaviors with those for whom they are providing peer support.
13. contact their clinical supervisor immediately with any perceived role conflict, ethical issue, or possible conflict of interest arising out of peer support.
14. seek immediate clinical supervision and consultation in any circumstance that reasonably exceeds the assessment and parameters of peer support.
15. reach out to others they know or suspect may benefit from peer support.
16. make reasonable effort to respond to individual requests for peer support and to respond to critical incidents as needed.
17. seek support from other peer support team members, their clinical supervisor, or other support personnel when stressed or otherwise in need of support.
18. are committed to helping other peer support persons to become better skilled. They do this by readily sharing their knowledge and experience when it does not conflict with the standards of peer support confidentiality.
19. endeavor to maintain a positive relationship with their clinical supervisor and other peer support team members, and make an effort to resolve any issues of conflict that may arise in these relationships.
20. understand that they are perceived as role models and that their actions reflect upon the entire team.
21. utilize self-enhancement peer support concepts in their personal lives.

(Digliani, J.A., 5/2015)

APPENDIX N

Examples of Police Peer Support Team Training Powerpoint Presentation

(reproduced in grayscale)

Clinical Supervision

Provides:

- Professional oversight
- Ladder of escalation with immediate supervision when necessary
- PST advanced training
- PST interaction resource
- Referral services
- Support for the supporters

Clinical supervision is established by policy, operational guidelines, and contract. There are two primary peer support supervision options: Advisor and Supervisor

---

Life by Design

and

Life by Default

Life by Default is what you get if you do not practice *Life by Design*
Consequence and "Prosequence"

Stage Model of Peer Support

Police Peer Support

- Stage I   *Exploration*
- Stage II *Person Objective Understanding*
- Stage III *Action Programs*

Egan, G. *The Skilled Helper* (2006)

Concepts
In
Police Peer Support

Useful Perspectives in Peer Support

Posttraumatic Responses and Posttraumatic Stress Disorder

Psychological Trauma

Peer Support and Peer Support
Intervention Strategies

Issues: Secondary injury and secondary traumatization

The "2 and 2"

The *2 and 2* is a useful way to think
about and cope with the emotional
experiences following a critical incident:

The first "2" - I know what this is – I
know what to do about it

The second "2" - Stronger and Smarter

Some Things to Remember

Outward Appearances

Peer support →

Field assessment →

Everyone has a private life
and some ability to look one
way and feel another.

Law Enforcement
Peer Support Team
Confidentiality

...before and after
C.R.S. 13-90-107(m)

...in states without
a peer support statute

Keeping
information
confidential is a
skill to be learned

Depression and the Brain

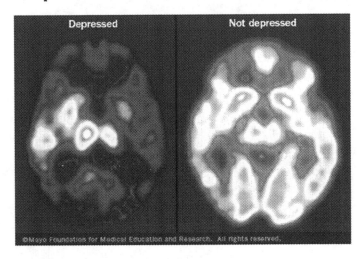

PET scan of the brains of a depressed
and not depressed person.

The
Make it Safe Police Officer Initiative
is aimed at reducing the
secondary danger of policing

Developed in 2013. J.A. Digliani

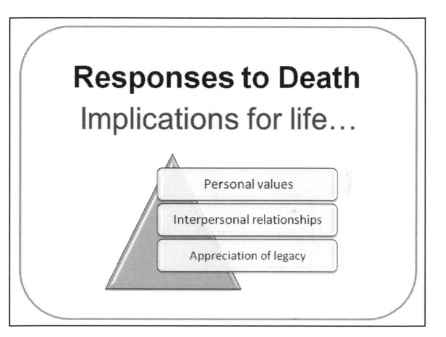

Responses to Death
Implications for life…

Personal values

Interpersonal relationships

Appreciation of legacy

Keeping Yourself Healthy

- Exercise regularly. Maintain an active lifestyle.
- Eat and drink a healthy diet.
- Maintain interests, hobbies, and relationships outside of policing.
- Do not hesitate to ask for support during stressful times.
- Practice what you have learned in PST training. No one is immune to stress.
- Utilize healthy stress management strategies that have worked for you .
- Experiment with new stressor management strategies.
- Maintain or reclaim your life, family, relationships, and career.
- Utilize and implement *Some Things to Remember*.
- Keep a positive attitude.
- Do not expect perfection – from yourself or others.
- Develop a sense of humor. Learn to laugh at yourself.
- Remain mindful of your personal boundaries.
- Apply and practice *life by design*.
- Support one another - seek support from other peer support team members.
- Remain mindful of *The Imperatives*.

ABOUT THE AUTHOR

Jack A. Digliani, PhD, EdD is a licensed psychologist and a former deputy sheriff, police officer, and detective. He served as a law enforcement officer for the Laramie County, Wyoming Sheriff's Office, the Cheyenne, Wyoming Police Department, and the Fort Collins, Colorado Police Services (FCPS). He was the FCPS Director of Human Services and police psychologist for the last 11 years of his FCPS police career. While in this position he provided psychological services to employees and their family, and clinically supervised the FCPS Peer Support Team. He received the FCPS Medal of Merit for his work in police psychology.

Dr. Digliani has also served as the police psychologist for the Loveland Police Department and Larimer County Sheriff's Office (Colorado). During this period of service, he provided psychological counseling services to department members and their families. He was also the clinical supervisor of the agencies' Peer Support Teams. He has worked with numerous municipal, county, state, and federal law enforcement agencies. He specializes in police and trauma psychology, group interventions, and the development of police, fire, and other emergency worker peer support teams.

Dr. Digliani is the author of Reflections of a Police Psychologist (now in 2nd edition), Police and Sheriff Peer Support Team Manual, Firefighter Peer Support Team Manual, Law Enforcement Critical Incident Handbook, and Law Enforcement Marriage and Relationship Guidebook. He is a contributor-writer of Colorado Revised Statute 13-90-107(m) *Who may not testify without consent*, the statute and paragraph which grants law enforcement, firefighter, and medical/

rescue peer support team members specified confidentiality protection during peer support interactions. He is also the primary author of the peer support section of the Officer-Involved Incident Protocol of the Eighth Judicial District of Colorado.

In 1990, Dr. Digliani created the Psychologist and Training/Recruit Officer Liaison (PATROL) program, a program designed to support new police officers and their families during academy and field training. This concept was later extended to the fire service. The Firefighter Recruit Support (FIRST) program supports firefighters and their families during recruit training.

In 1992, Dr. Digliani developed the Freezeframe method of critical incident debriefing. As a result of his many years of experience, he conceptualized the police option-funnel versus threat-funnel, Level I and Level II peer support, the Proactive Annual Check-in, and the Comprehensive Model for Police Advanced Strategic Support (COMPASS). This strategic program was later extended to firefighters in the Comprehensive Model for Peer Advanced Strategic Support. COMPASS is a career-long psychological health and wellness strategy for police officers and firefighters. In 2013, Dr. Digliani developed the conceptions of primary and secondary danger. He then created the Make it Safe Police Officer Initiative, a 12-element strategy designed to reduce the secondary danger of policing. This was extended to the fire service in the Make it Safe Firefighter Initiative.

REFERENCES

American Psychiatric Association. (1952). *Diagnostic and statistical manual of mental disorders*. Washington, DC: Author.

American Psychiatric Association. (1980). *Diagnostic and statistical manual of mental disorders* (3rd ed.). Washington, DC: Author.

American Psychiatric Association. (1987). *Diagnostic and statistical manual of mental disorders* (3rd ed., revised). Washington, DC: Author.

American Psychiatric Association. (1994). *Diagnostic and statistical manual of mental disorders* (4th ed.). Washington, DC: Author.

American Psychiatric Association. (2000). *Diagnostic and statistical manual of mental disorders*. (4th ed., text revision). Washington, DC: Author.

American Psychiatric Association. (2013). *Diagnostic and statistical manual of mental disorders* (5th ed.). Washington, DC: Author.

Artwohl, A. & Christensen, L.W. (1997). *Deadly force encounters*. Boulder: Paladin Press.

Barton, R. (2011). *Counselling skills: A five minute training course*. Retrieved 2011 from https://www.youtube.com/watch?v=I9RuMujWhXY.

Berne, E. (1964). *Games people play – the basic hand book of transactional analysis.* New York: Ballantine Books.

Digliani, J.A. (2015). *Reflections of a police psychologist (2nd ed).* New Jersey: Xlibris.

Digliani, J.A. (1992). *Guidelines for conducting a police critical incident debriefing.* Unpublished manuscript.

Egan, G. (2006). *The skilled helper: A problem-management and opportunity-development approach to helping.* Brooks/Cole: Belmont, CA.

Harris, T.A. (1967). *I'm ok - you're ok.* New York: Harper Collins.

Herman, J. (2015). *Trauma and recovery: The aftermath of violence--from domestic abuse to political terror.* New York: Basic Books.

James, M. & Jongeward, D. (1978). *Born to win: Transactional analysis with gestalt experiments.* New York: New American Library.

Koolhaas, J.M., Bartolomucci, A., Buwalda, B., de Boer, S.F., Flugge, G., Korte, S.M., Meerlo, P., Murison, R., Olivier, B., Palanza, P., Richter-Levin, G., Sgoifo, A., Steimer, T., Stiedl, O., van Dijk, G., Wohr, M., & Fuchs, E.. (2011). Stress revisited: A critical evaluation of the stress concept. *Neuroscience and Biobehavioral Reviews,* 35, 1291–1301.

Lewin, K. Z. (1943). Defining the "Field at a Given Time." *Psychological Review.* 50: 292-310. Republished in *Resolving Social Conflicts & Field Theory in Social Science,* Washington, D.C: American Psychological Association, 1997.

McLeod, S. A. (2008). *Person centered therapy.* Retrieved 2009 from http://www.simplypsychology.org/client-centred-therapy.html)

Meier, S.T. & Davis, S.R. (2011) *The elements of counseling*, 7th ed. Brooks/Cole: Belmont, CA.

Meyers, R. J. (2014) *CRAFT: An alternative to intervention*. Retrieved 2014 from http://www.robertjmeyersphd.com/craft.html.

Miller, W. R. and Rollnick, S. (1991) *Motivational interviewing: Preparing people to change addictive behavior*. New York: Guilford Press.

Mitchell, J.T. (1983). When disaster strikes...the critical incident stress debriefing process. *Journal of Emergency Medical Services*, 8(1): 36-39.

Mitchell, J.T. & Everly, G.S. (1996). *Critical incident stress debriefing: an operations manual*. Ellicott City, MD: Chevron.

Mohandie, K., Meloy, J.R., & Collins, P. I. (2009). Suicide by cop among officer-involved shooting cases. *Journal of Forensic Sciences*, 54 (2) 456-462.

Rieser, M. (1973). Practical psychology for police officers. Springfiled, IL: C.C. Thomas.

Richardson, D. (2010). *Counselling roleplay - reflecting, paraphrasing and summarising*. Retrieved 2011 from https://www.youtube.com/watch?v=2aRq1LC05-A.

Rogers, C. (1961) *On becoming a person: A therapist's view of psychotherapy*. New York: Houghton-Mifflin.

Rothlin, P. & and Werder, P. (2008). *Boreout! Overcoming workplace demotivation*. London: Kogan Page Limited.

Selye, H. (1974). *Stress without distress*. New York: Signet.

Steiner, C. (1990). *Scripts people live: Transactional analysis of life scripts*. New York: Grove Press.

Straker, G. (1987). The continuous traumatic stress syndrome: The single therapeutic interview. *Psychology in Society* (8): 46–79.

Violanti, J.M., O'Hara, A.F., & Tate, T.T. (2011). *On the edge: Recent perspectives on police suicide*. Springfield, IL: Charles C. Thomas.

Worden, J.W. (2008). *Grief Counseling and Grief Therapy: A handbook for the mental health practitioner.* New York: Springer.

Zimbardo, P., Sword, R., Sword, R. (2012). *The time cure: Overcoming PTSD with the new psychology of time perspective therapy*. San Francisco: Jossey-Bass.

INDEX

A

acute stress disorder, 53
adjustment disorder, 53
alcohol, 19, 40, 46, 49, 83-91, 98,
    108, 131, 194-195, 209
    addiction, 84-91
    use disorder, 85
Alcoholics anonymous, 20, 88
alcoholism, 86-87
    warning signs, 86
anger, 40, 61
appropriate assertiveness, 121,
    150-153

B

behaviorism, 71,
Below 100 initiative, 123-129
bipolar disorder, 92-93, 100
boreout, 19, 39-40
brief psychotic disorder, 53
burnout, 19, 39-40

C

clinical supervision, 3, 5, 22, 68-
    70, 139
peer support team, 1-13, 14-27,
    44, 53, 63-70, 102, 118, 131,
    134, 163-165, 170-177, 178-
    205, 216-217
code of ethical conduct, 216
cognitive behavioral therapy, 54,
    71, 73
communication imperative, 35, 37
community reinforcement and
family training (CRAFT), 87, 89
confidentiality, 4-10, 64-71, 172,
    204, 216
    federal court system, 11-12, 65
    waiver, 65-66
confrontation,
Comprehensive model for police
advanced strategic support
(COMPASS), 102, 128, 133, 212
communicate to motivate, 153
communication, 21, 35, 112, 115,
    180
    interpersonal, 35
    tips, 36

conceptualization, 37-39, 45, 51,
    71
couples, 43-46, 157-160
    and money, 159-160
confessions, 66
criminal, 66
critical incident, 21-22, 47-108,
    186-191
criticism, 63, 86,
    and police action, 147

D

death, 28, 48, 93, 98-104
    loss and survivorship, 110
diagnosis, 45-50
Diagnostic and Statistical Manual
of Mental Disorders, 45, 52, 151,
    182
debriefing, 118-121
depression, 51, 79, 90-94, 100,
    160, 209-210
drugs, 40, 84-86, 210
Drunkards Club, 20
duty to warn, 66

E

ego state, 112
elements, 109, 121,
    of Make it Safe Police Officer
    Initiative, 133-134

F

family, 41-45
    dynamics, 41

issues, 41
    types, 43
foundation blocks of
functional relationships, 43,
    178-181
free money, 159-160

G

grief, 109-112

H

hallucination, 51, 54
harm, 42, 59, 90, 119
    intentional, 42-43
    unintentional, 42-43
humanistic-existential, 54, 71, 74
helper principle, 20
helping a person that is suicidal,
    99, 209

I

implementation, 109
    of Make it Safe Police Officer
    Initiative, 135-140
intellectual disability, 45-47
investigations, 63
    administrative, 63-64
    criminal, 63-64

J

judged by the outcome, 148-150

K

keeping yourself healthy, 121

L

Law Enforcement Marriage and
Relationship Guidebook, 26, 44
Law Enforcement Critical Incident
Handbook, 26, 57, 108
Level I peer support, 6-7, 20
Level II peer support, 2, 6-7, 20
licensed clinicians, 9
life by default, 38-39
life by design, 38-39
line of duty, 124, 126, 128
    death, 100
    injury, 126

M

make a contact everyday (MACE),
    25
Make it Safe Police Officer
Initiative, 102, 108
    and administrators, 145
    and officers, 143
    implementation, 135
mania, 92-93
Marriage and Couples Exercise,
    158
medication, 10, 46, 49
mental health, 19, 45, 98
mental illness, 19, 45
    treatments, 45-46, 90
model for peer support, 7
motivation deflation, 153

motivational interviewing, 15, 90
mourning, 109

N

neurobiological, 84
    drug addiction, 84

O

occupational imperative, 32
officer's dilemma, 148
officer wellness assessment, 191
option funnel-threat funnel, 63
organizational climate, 108, 142
other people are not you, 155

P

passive aggression, 150
patterns of behavior, 157
peer support tips, 80
Police and Sheriff Peer Support
Team Manual, 20, 78
police officer suicide risk factors,
    100
Police Peer Support Team Training
    program, 16
prosequence, 39
psychologist and training/recruit
officer liaison (PATROL), 21, 166
peer support team, 14, 21-27
posttraumatic stress disorder, 47,
    50-53, 182
power of the peer, 1
primary danger, 126,
    physical, 127

psychological, 127-128
Proactive Annual Check-in, 34,
    102
psychiatrist, 10
psychoanalysis, 54, 71
psychologist, 8-10, 34, 47, 126
psychotherapy, 10, 20

Q

question, persuade, refer (QPR),
    98-99

R

rational-emotive behavioral
therapy, 54, 79-80, 206
reach out, 24-27, 102
referral, 7, 70, 90
Reflections of a Police
Psychologist, 57, 111
relationship imperative, 33, 44, 157
return to duty protocol, 56-57, 191

S

safety net, 82
schedules of reinforcement, 72
second injury, 59, 139, 186
secondary danger, 108, 123,
    128-130
secondary trauma, 60, 132
self-initiated peer support activity
(SPA), 25
self-management for addiction
recovery (SMART), 89

silent treatment, 42, 150
shock, impact, recovery, 58
some things to remember, 32, 122
stress, 27-35
    deprivational, 29
    overload, 28
stressor, 27-35
suicidality, 161,
suicide by cop, 104
support for the supporters, 22, 26,
    139
surface lesson-deep lesson, 49,
    62

T

three "seconds" of policing, 132
time machine, 63-64
tips, 36, 80
tactics and technology, 126
transactional analysis, 112-116
trauma, 47-58
Trauma Intervention Program, 54,
    187-189
traumatic incident, 47-58
    factors affecting, 50
    responses following, 49
tunnel, 60
    feeling, 60, 160-162
    thinking, 60, 160-162
    vision, 49, 160-162
twelve steps, 87
    of AA, 87-88
two and two, 34, 53, 63-64

U

United Order of Ex-Boozers, 20

V

validation-invalidation, 36
vivid images, 49

W

walk and talk, 34, 55, 62, 64
witness to suicide, 104-108

Printed in the United States
By Bookmasters